1195

# The Pelican Guide
## to
# New Orleans

*Touring America's Most Interesting City*

## THOMAS K. GRIFFIN
*Introduction by Mayor Sidney Barthelemy*

## Pelican Publishing Company
### Gretna 1988

First edition, October 1962
Second edition, September 1974
Third edition, January 1978
Fourth edition, November 1980
Fifth edition, January 1983
Sixth edition, October 1983
Seventh edition, January 1988

*For my late mother*
JENNIE KURTZ GRIFFIN
*Without whom, obviously,*
*this could never have been written*

**Library of Congress Cataloging-in-Publication Data**

Griffin, Thomas Kurtz.
    The Pelican guide to New Orleans.

    Includes index.
        1. New Orleans (La.)—Description—Guide-books.
I. Title.
F379.N53G74      1988      917.63'350463      87-7338
ISBN 0-88289-684-9

Information in this guidebook is based on authoritative data at
the time of printing. Prices and hours of operation of businesses
listed are subject to change without notice. Readers are asked to
take this into account when consulting this guide.

Manufactured in the United States of America
Published by Pelican Publishing Company, Inc.
1101 Monroe Street, Gretna, Louisiana 70053

# Contents

# CITY OF NEW ORLEANS
## OFFICE OF THE MAYOR

Sidney J. Barthelemy
Mayor

## G R E E T I N G S

As Mayor of the City of New Orleans, it is an honor and privilege to present the <u>Pelican Guide to New Orleans</u> by Tommy Griffin, a long-time newspaper man and columnist, well-known to many of our citizens. The Guide is a current collection of attractions, eating establishments and places to see in our own Crescent City.

Touring the City of New Orleans is a fun-filled experience for the whole family, and this collection serves as a valuable guide to experiencing the charm, tradition and excitement New Orleans has to offer.

From the New Orleans Museum of Art and the French Quarter Festival to the Riverwalk shopping development, New Orleans is a mosaic of creole heritage and insightful innovation.

Whether a native New Orleanian or a first-time visitor, the <u>Pelican Guide to New Orleans</u> is a book to be read over and over again.

Sincerely,

Sidney J. Barthelemy
Mayor

# THE PELICAN GUIDE TO
# NEW ORLEANS

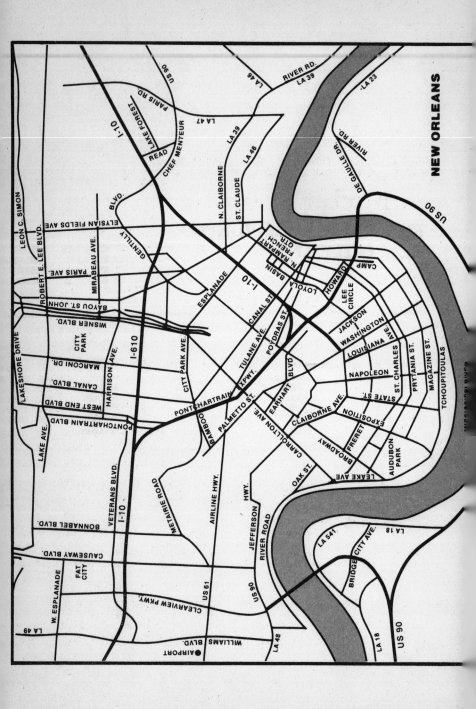

# NEW ORLEANS

# 1

# NEW ORLEANS: America's Most Interesting City

New Orleans is a crazy, mixed-up, wonderful, romantic, historic, modern bit of geography located on a crescent bend of the Mississippi River, 110 miles from the Gulf of Mexico. The city of New Orleans has a unique and colorful history. She was founded by Jean Baptiste le Moyne, Sieur de Bienville, as a French colony in 1718, but was ruled by the Spanish from 1762 to 1803 when she was returned to France by Spain. In 1803, Napoleon sold New Orleans and the whole Louisiana Territory, which now comprises all or part of thirteen states, to the United States for fifteen million dollars, in what has been called the greatest real estate bargain in history.

New Orleans is one of the largest cities in land area in the United States, but 166 of its 365 square miles are under water. Levees keep the river out, but rainfall is so heavy, particularly in summer, that a system of pumping stations has to be maintained to pump the water into

canals that carry it into Lake Pontchartrain, which bounds
the city on the north.

New Orleans clings to her gracious traditions of the
past while keeping pace with the present and planning
for the future. One streetcar line remains for auld lang
syne. It rumbles along St. Charles Avenue and Carrollton
Avenue and touches Canal Street for only one block. The
Canal Street trolleys were removed from the city's main
thoroughfare (171 feet wide and reputedly one of the
widest and best-lighted streets in the country) on May 31,
1964, despite strong opposition by a group of citizens
banded together under the colorful name of "Streetcars
Desired, Inc."

Horse-and-buggy tours are still available for a trip
through the French Quarter, and six excursion riverboats
ply the "Mighty Mississippi" on daylight and moonlight
cruises. The riverboat *Natchez* (capacity 1,600) makes three
trips a day at 11:30 A.M. and 2:30 and 6:30 P.M.; the
latter is a dinner cruise nightly. The riverboat *Bayou Jean
Lafitte,* (capacity 600) makes a daily bayou cruise from 11
A.M. to 4 P.M. with full galley facilities for luncheon on
board. A new cruise, originated in 1982 by the same
company, is a shuttle service from the Canal Street dock
to the Audubon Park Zoo three times daily by the riverboat *Cotton Blossom* (capacity 300). Departure times from
Canal Street are 10 A.M. and 12:45 and 3:30 P.M. Return
trips from the zoo depart at 11:30 A.M. and 2:15 and 5
P.M. The boat returns to Canal Street at 5:45 P.M.

The S.S. *President* (capacity 3,100), largest of the Mississippi fleet of the New Orleans riverboats, sails only on
Friday and Saturday nights, frequently with special attractions and big name stars. The ship cruises from 10 P.M.
to midnight, and remains dockside until 1 A.M. at Canal
Street. (The *Natchez* and *Bayou Jean Lafitte* depart from
and return to the Toulouse Street wharf.)

There is another bayou cruise called the *Voyageur*, privately owned by Robert Spangenberg, Sr. (capacity 183). It also traverses the river en route to Bayou Barataria, one of Louisiana's most fascinating and mysterious waterways. This is a five-hour trip departing at 10 A.M. from Canal Street. Poor boy sandwiches are served on board. The *Voyageur* is the only bayou cruise boat that offers its passengers the "lagniappe" (loosely translated—"a little something extra") of visiting the historic Chalmette Battlefield where Gen. Andrew Jackson defeated the British in the Battle of New Orleans in 1815.

The latest addition to the New Orleans fleet of riverboats is the *Creole Queen*, christened on September 11, 1983. This paddlewheeler has three decks and a capacity of 1,000 passengers. It measures 190 feet from stem to stern and is 40 feet wide. There are two daylight cruises at 10 A.M. and 2 P.M. with boarding 30 minutes before departure. There is also a dinner cruise at 8 P.M. with boarding at 7 P.M. The *Creole Queen* docks at the Poydras Street Wharf.

The riverboat *Natchez* berthed along the river adjacent to the newly-renovated Jackson Brewery.

The same company, New Orleans Paddlewheels, Inc., expects to add another riverboat, the *Cajun Queen*, in the very near future.

New Orleans International Airport, dedicated late in 1959, recently added twenty new gates and extended the north-south and east-west runways to accommodate the latest type of aircraft. The airport was one of the first in the United States to accommodate the supersonic transport *Concorde* during the Bicentennial visit of President Giscard d'Estaing of France to New Orleans.

Work began recently at the airport to extend the western runway 1,200 feet into the adjacent marshlands. When completed, this will enable the airport to accommodate even larger jumbo jets, in addition to carrying much of the noise and potential danger away from the densely-populated surrounding neighborhoods. Other noticeable improvements to the airport terminal facilities are being made as well.

The Union Passenger Terminal for rail travelers, completed in 1954 and one of the first air-conditioned railroad terminals in the nation, is also being used as a terminal for bus passengers because of the decline in rail travel in recent years. Amtrak, however, is trying to correct that problem and signs of progress do appear. Meanwhile, there's also talk of converting the terminal into a Transportation Center that will include accommodations for the airlines.

New Orleans also has a comparatively new Civic Center which has replaced an old slum area in the midtown section. The cluster of new buildings on the fourteen-acre site includes the city hall, the state office building, the state supreme court building, the civil courts building, the main branch of the public library, and a U.S. post office. The latter opened on April 1, 1962.

There's a Mississippi River Bridge (currently toll free in the business section), which was "floated" by a $65 million

bond issue, and dedicated on October 18, 1958. Work on
another badly needed bridge is now underway 400 feet
downstream from the present span—after a controversy
of more than a dozen years.

Spanning Lake Pontchartrain, the world's longest
causeway—almost twenty-four miles long—links the city
with the piney woods of St. Tammany Parish.

New Orleans can have several varieties of climate in a
single day. Temperatures of seventy degrees or higher
have been recorded every month, with one exception,
since the National Weather Bureau opened here on October 24, 1870. The exception was January, 1872, when the
mercury got no higher than sixty-eight degrees. Flowers
bloom the year around, but your bones can tingle in any
month from December through March—the humidity
does it. You can be uncomfortably hot in New Orleans at
eighty-five degrees, uncomfortably cold at forty. Shirt-
sleeve weather and freezing temperatures have been known
to occur in a twenty-four-hour period in mid-winter,
when rains chase away the sunshine. If you plan to visit
the city during the winter months, bring several weights
of clothes.

New Orleans is both naughty and nice. It is a churchgoing
city; and a fun-loving city. The populace, more than half
of it Catholic parades to church each Sunday, no matter
how much wassail it consumed the night before. Denomi-
nations are plentiful—the city boasts more than six hundred churches to worship in as you choose.

There is no curfew on drinking. You may buy liquor
across a bar at any hour of the day or night, weekday or
Sunday. But watch it! Police are cracking down on DWI
offenders—driving while intoxicated. They're pretty tolerant, however, of pedestrians if they're not disturbing
the peace.

Basin Street is no longer the street of sin. Time has
transported much of its activity to Bourbon Street in the

French Quarter, Basin, fabled in song and the history of jazz, is now a respectable midtown boulevard. A government housing project stands where the red-light district once flourished, and three statues dedicated to Latin American heroes decorate the street's broad neutral ground.

New Orleans is among the top twenty-five cities in the United States in population, but like most cities, the urban area is losing residents to the suburbs. The 1980 census lists Orleans Parish (the city proper) as having 557,482 people. The Greater New Orleans area population, which includes the parishes of Jefferson, St. Bernard, and St. Tammany, is given as 1,182,725. The population of New Orleans is now more than 50 percent black.

The latest count of hotel and motel accommodations lists about 26,000 rooms in the city area.

Until recent years, almost all of the exclusive dress shops and departments stores were located on or near Canal Street, but no longer. Traffic congestion and lack of adequate parking facilities caused a number of these stores to move to sparkling new buildings along a recently-renovated riverfront. Such famous names as Saks Fifth Avenue, Gucci's, Brooks Brothers, etc. are now located in new shopping centers with names like Canal Place, the Jackson Brewery, Uptown Square, and the Rouse Corporations's Riverwalk. High quality dress shops can also be found as far uptown as the 2200-block of St. Charles Avenue.

Still other stores have moved to or opened branches in huge shopping malls in eastern New Orleans such as the Plaza in Lake Forest, just off I-10 at Read Boulevard. Shopping malls are also flourishing in the surrounding suburban areas.

New Orleans is famed for food and drink. Her chefs are noted for the small miracles they create by adding piquant sauces to the native fish and game which abound in the waters and marshlands. Her bartenders have popularized such famous thirst-quenchers as the Sazerac cocktail, the Ramos gin fizz, the Hurricane rum drink, and the absinthe frappé—now served with Pernod or Herbsaint.

New Orleans is known for her distinctive architecture—the French Quarter buildings, not wholly French or Spanish but a blend of the two, with modifications made necessary by local climatic and topographic conditions; the first American homes in the Garden District, dozens of big houses containing twenty or thirty rooms, constructed in an odd fusion of classic styles, including Greek Revival; and the plantation homes still standing along the banks of Bayou St. John on Moss Street.

New Orleans has sights that burn into the memory: sunsets over the gabled roofs of the French Quarter, viewed from the center of Jackson Square; the swirling muddy waters of the mighty Mississippi that have inspired so many stories, poems, and songs; the panorama of the city from the rotating cocktail lounge of the World Trade Center Tower, thirty-three stories high; Canal Street on a rainy night, when the wet asphalt mirrors the kaleidoscope colors of the neon signs. And there is one special sight in which Orleanians delight: Monkey Hill in Audubon Park. This was an 18-foot high creation of mud dredged from the lagoons so the children of New Orleans would know what a hill looks like. The rest of the town is so flat, kids scamper over Monkey Hill as if they were scaling Mount Everest. Leveled during recent park improvements a new Monkey Hill has grown to even greater height (28 feet).

New Orleans has odd names for streets. Her French and Spanish rulers, Catholic to the core, expressed their faith when they named Assumption, Piety, Annunciation, Religious, Ursulines, Ascension, St. Peter, St. Ann, St. Philip, St. Roch, and St. Claude. Greek classical influence is shown by such street names as Calliope, Euterpe, Terpsichore, Melpomene, Polymnia, Erato, Urania, Thalia, Homer, Socrates, Ptolemy, Coliseum, and Dryades. Indian tribes were honored in the naming of Tchoupitoulas, Chippewa, Teche, Cherokee, Seminole, and Natchez. Moral and fanciful thoughts are expressed by Mystery, Industry, Humanity, Pleasure, Genius, Virtue, and Desire.

Ironically, the street named St. Claude crosses both Piety and Desire—the latter, of course, was made famous by playwright Tennessee Williams in *A Streetcar Named Desire*. A bus has now replaced the streetcar for transit service, but one remnant of the Desire line remains. It's a museum piece: a freshly painted, completely restored streetcar bearing the sign *Desire*. It stands in the courtyard of the old U.S. Mint, opposite the French Market, near the corner of Barracks and Decatur streets.

New Orleans is the gateway for the midwestern area of the United States to ports in Central and South America, the West Indies, and the world. Her docks are always lined with ships flying flags of many countries. Facilities for passenger cruises from New Orleans to ports in Mexico, Central America, and the Caribbean are available from a cruise ship terminal in the Rivercenter Complex, which includes the New Orleans Hilton Hotel.

New Orleans is a "good neighbor" to international businessmen. The World Trade Center, located on the riverfront at Canal Street, is open to the public. It is a center of trade from which manufacturers may sell in both domestic and foreign markets.

New Orleans borders a bit on the bizarre. It is a city where the name of Jean Lafitte, a pirate, is revered; where a traffic safety island or median is a "neutral ground;" where a square named Lafayette has three statues on pedestals, but none of Lafayette. (The statues immortalize the memories of Benjamin Franklin, Henry

Clay, and John McDonogh. McDonogh was a bachelor all Orleanians considered the tightest of misers until he died; then he bequeathed enough money to the school children of New Orleans to build thirty-five public schools.)

New Orleans is a city where the north side is downtown instead of uptown; where the sun rises on the west bank of the Mississippi and sinks again in the west, in Jefferson Parish (because of the bend in the river); where the city streets—with the exception of those in the French Quarter— in trying to follow the course of the river, wind and twine into a pattern resembling the figure eight (did you ever try to find a direction on a figure eight?)

In New Orleans, a woman makes a livelihood teaching Mardi Gras queens how to flourish their scepters and walk with grace while bearing heavy mantles trailing from their shoulders; where costume makers are busy all year round designing and sewing silks and satins for the more than sixty Carnival balls held each season; where float-building is a specialized, profitable enterprise; where more gentlemen wear formal clothes than in any other city in the United States.

In this city, even dignitaries are not immune from calling up an illegal bookie to lay a wager if they get a hot tip on a horse; and the faithful insert classified ads in the newspapers to show their gratitude to the saints ("Thanks to St. Jude for a favor granted").

New Orleans is sometimes called "The City Care Forgot" because of her unhurried, capricious mode of living; she is sometimes called "The Paris of America" because of her Old World customs and charm; and she is frequently called the "Crescent City" because of the crescent bend of the river. But the slogan with which I agree is "America's Most Interesting City." Y'all come and see for yourself!

The new Place St. Charles contrasts with the old architectural style of the French Quarter. *(Courtesy Greater
New Orleans Tourist & Convention Commission)*

# 2
# What Makes
# New Orleans Interesting

When General Charles de Gaulle president of France, visited New Orleans on April 29, 1960, he recalled, "Before the United States came into existence as a nation, there were French achievements on the banks of the Mississippi. Seeds were planted, and thanks to those seeds, your city still bears some of the marks of France."

Others have felt a similar rapport with the city on first sight. The late Cornelius Vanderbilt, Jr., world traveler, socialite, author, and columnist, said that what he liked about New Orleans is its love of tradition: "No other American city is as justly proud of its heritage or adheres more closely to a gracious mode of living."

Zsa Zsa Gabor rates it her favorite American city because, "It is the most European of all American cities, not alone for its architecture but also because of the people's attitude toward life, the way they take time to pursue the science of living."

Joan Crawford found a "magnetic charm never to be

forgotten" in the way "New Orleans so well combines the atmosphere of the Old World with the new."

Lucius Beebe, the late dilettante, once observed over a gleaming glass of champagne: "It seems to me more people get more enjoyment out of good food in New Orleans than in any other city in the United States. New York may have a few finer restaurants, but only the rich can afford the prices. In New Orleans all levels of society make a cult of appreciation of good food, and woe to any restaurant that doesn't serve it."

"It's Paris, America, and the Caribbean all in one!" Joan Fontaine exclaimed. "If I had a choice of a place to live, I'd choose New Orleans."

"It has an appeal, a kind of charm. It seems as though I've been here before," is the way Louis Vaudable, owner of Maxim's in Paris, put it.

We are proud of these opinions and, of course, agree wholeheartedly with them. But what makes our city so different?

New Orleans was a Latin city a century old before it became part of the United States. The Creoles were proud of being foreigners and first settlers when the first Americans moved in after the Louisiana Purchase from France in 1803. The Creoles were then firmly entrenched in the French Quarter, so the Americans built their homes and business establishments on the other side of what was supposed to be a navigation canal on the southern boundary of the Quarter. That canal was never built, but today a drainage canal flows a short distance under Canal Street. And the street is still the dividing line between the old and new sections of the city.

The upper side of Canal Street embodies the city's progress, its tall buildings, financial center, and seat of government. The lower side, the French Quarter, contains the quaint, ancient buildings, the historic points of interest, the museums, the artists' colony, the antique and curio shops, the famous restaurants, and a nightclub row reminiscent of Montmartre. It is to the French Quarter that most tourists flock—where they meet the most interesting people, including Orleanians.

There's really nothing quite like an Orleanian. He speaks a language all his own. An attuned ear can detect several dialects in various parts of the city, but two varieties predominate. One can only be described as southern Brooklynese. It is heard all over town except in the Garden District and university section. *Oil* is pronounced *erl,* *turn* becomes *toin,* and *the* is *de.* Residents of the Garden District and the university section speak an admixture of the king's English with a southern accent. But even within this group there is a discernible distinction between the articulation of women and men. A woman is likely to speak more like her forebears in the southern tradition. A man, because of his business affiliations in the vast Mississippi Valley, has something of a midwestern tone to his talk. The language on the whole seems to have evolved from the blending of a typical southern plantation dialect with a number of non-English-speaking groups. Thus it's not uncommon for an Orleanian to refer to a sidewalk as a banquette, or a porch as a gallery.

When giving geographical instructions, an Orleanian never uses such hackneyed points of the compass as north, south, east, and west. How could he when the bend of the river precludes any clear-cut pattern of streets? Consequently, he uses the river, the lake, uptown, and downtown in "clearly" pointing out to strangers—as well as natives—how to reach any given destination. If, for example, you are seeking the Cabildo, the ancient seat of the Spanish government which is now a part of the Louisiana State Museum, you are likely to be told, "You can't miss it; it's on the downtown-lake corner of St. Peter

and Chartres Streets, opposite Jackson Square." And if
you are as confused by that as I might be in any strange
town, you'd be wise to call a cab and simply say, "The
Cabildo, please!" You can't miss it.

The alternative is to follow the walking-tour map of the
Quarter which is available free at hotel and motel desks.
You really ought to strike out on your own with a map.
You'll find it a quite interesting stroll as well as a compar-
atively easy thing to do, for the streets in the French
Quarter are the only ones in town that are laid out in a
perfect square.

Is an Orleanian really a stickler for tradition? A decade
or more ago when the Dinkler Hotel chain bought the
venerable St. Charles Hotel (established in 1836), the new
management removed an outdated brass plaque reading
"Ladies' Entrance" on one of the three entrances to the
hotel. Such a howl was raised by the citizenry to restore
the quaint little sign that Carling Dinkler, Jr., relented
and had it replaced, accompanied by much fanfare in the
press. The hotel is now demolished and a large office
building has replaced it.

Even a hint of changing the status of a historic building
is likely to rouse the populace. Not long ago a rumor
gained headway that the city of New Orleans was considering selling the upper Pontalba apartment building fronting
on Jackson Square which, with its identical companion
building on the opposite side of the Square, claims the
distinction of being the first apartment houses in the
United States. To protest against such a horror, a mass
meeting was called by the Louisiana Landmarks Society,
headed by New Orleans author Harnett Kane as program
chairman. The turnout on a rainy, wintry night included
solid citizens of several organizations dedicated to the
preservation of the French Quarter and ready to do
battle with City Hall. But the meeting turned out to be an
anticlimax when the incumbent Mayor deLesseps S.

Morrison wired the group that there had never been any truth in the rumor.

Equally as strong as the determination to preserve the city's architectural heritage is the determination of New Orleans socialites that their city remain the last stronghold of traditional society in the United States. Thus an Orleanian's status in the social register is based primarily on lineage rather than the acquisition of wealth in the business world or personal accomplishment in the arts. The hard core of New Orleans society is composed of many families in the middle-income bracket, plus a few on whom hard times have brought comparative poverty. Yet their pride in their heritage is such that they cling to the grandeur of their "names" and the preservation of their old homes, which have been handed down to them from generation to generation. One frequently hears stories of an impoverished family pawning its jewels in order that a daughter or granddaughter might make her debut for to make one's debut, and to be queen of a Carnival ball is more important to one's pride than meeting next week's grocery bills.

And groceries, or the delights of the table—evaluated earlier in Lucius Beebe's remark—are dear to the hearts of all Orleanians. For in New Orleans dining is a function instead of a chore, and cooking has reached a degree of perfection unattained elsewhere in this country. The late Dorothy Dix, an adopted Orleanian, once declared: "Tourists come as definitely to New Orleans to eat as they go to New York to see the plays or to Washington to behold the seat of government, or to Hollywood to gape at the movie stars."

New Orleans abounds in legends. A legend may be true, but it's different from a fact; documentary evidence may be fragmentary. Consequently, some of the tales the natives spin are part fact, part fiction.

There is a mitigating factor. Confusion is likely to arise

in any populace when one is faced with the problem of explaining two Napoleon houses, two Beauregard houses, two Old Absinthe House bars, and two Café Lafittes—one "in exile."

Although sightseeing guides generally point out a three-story building of stuccoed brick with a cupola at top, located at 500 Chartres Street, as the Napoleon House, Napoleon never lived there. In fact, he never set foot in New Orleans. He died of cancer in his fifty-third year on May 5, 1821, in exile on the island of St. Helena. He had previously been exiled to the island of Elba, and his escape from there is what gives rise to the speculation as to which is the Napoleon House—the building at 500 Chartres Street which is now a bar and restaurant, or a building at 514 Chartres Street which is now a pharmaceutical museum.

Mayor Nicholas Girod, who was in office during that period, was involved with both houses. When news of Napoleon's escape was published in the *Louisiana Gazette* on May 25, 1811, the leading citizens were enjoying a play at the St. Philip Theatre (later the Washington Ballroom). Everyone was sure Napoleon would head for New Orleans, where he'd feel comfortably at home. Mayor Girod was so enthused he made a speech declaring he'd place his private residence at 500 Chartres Street at the disposal of the beloved emperor. Thus the building became known as the Napoleon House.

The second Napoleon House has another story. The legend is that it was erected and furnished with funds supplied by Mayor Girod during Napoleon's second exile, on St. Helena. The mayor had made plans with Dominique You, one of the pirate Lafitte's top lieutenants, to kidnap and rescue the emperor and transport him secretly to New Orleans. The plot involved sailing a fast schooner, manned by a daredevil crew, across the Atlantic to abduct

Old Absinthe House, at the corner of Bienville and Bourbon. Its namesake, the Old Absinthe House Bar, operates a block down the street, a confusing situation resulting from the temporary closure of the original during Prohibition. *(Courtesy Louisiana Office of Tourism)*

the imperial prisoner. But just as the ship was about to sail, news of Napoleon's death quashed the whole scheme.

Of the two buildings, the one at 500 Chartres Street appears to have more claim to its name, inasmuch as Mayor Girod was the prime mover in instigating plans to transport Napoleon to New Orleans.

The two homes accredited to General P. G. T. Beauregard, under whose command the first shots of the Civil War were fired on Fort Sumter, are equivocal. The one at 1113 Chartres Street is more generally accepted today as the Beauregard House. It is presently owned by the Frances Parkinson Keyes Foundation. Mrs. Keyes, a world-famous novelist, occupied the house for years until her death on July 3, 1970. One of her novels, *Madame Castel's Lodger,* deals with the time Beauregard spent at the Chartres Street address. She bequeathed the house to the Keyes Foundation, of which Lloyd W. Huber is the current president. The house is open to tourists weekdays from 10 A.M. to 4 P.M. Advance notice is required for large groups.

Historians, however, claim Beauregard resided there only several months in rented rooms, whereas he and his son lived for many years after the Civil War at 934 Royal Street. His birthplace is said by some historians to have been a community named Contreras, six miles from New Orleans in St. Bernard Parish, which boasted a population of fifty persons at that time. Beauregard died in another home, 1631 Esplanade Avenue, on February 20, 1893.

The confusion of the Old Absinthe House and the Old Absinthe House Bar, within a block of each other on Bourbon Street, is more fun to explain. Paradoxically, both are entitled to the claim of original. During Prohibition the original Old Absinthe House on Bourbon and Bienville streets, built in the early nineteenth century, was

Blacksmith shop reputed to have been used by pirate
Jean Lafitte. *(Courtesy Louisiana Office of Tourism)*

operated as a speakeasy by one Pierre Cazebonne. In
1924 it was raided by federal agents who padlocked the
doors. But one dark night someone forced an entry
through the rear of the building and carried out the bar,
the cash register, and the paintings on the walls. Not long
afterward a new speakeasy opened at the next corner, at
Bourbon and Conti streets. Coincidentally, Pierre Cazebonne
turned up as proprietor. Came repeal, and the original
house was at one corner the original bar at the other. It's
this peculiar set of circumstances that flabbergasts tourists
on first sight. When they run into the second bar after
seeing the first, they think it's a hoax. Actually both are
historically correct.

About ten years ago, the original Old Absinthe House,
because of its crumbling antiquity, underwent a face-

lifting. The building was gutted and rebuilt in elegance.
The exterior, conforming to Vieux Carré Commission
regulations, remains much the same as it was. On the
other hand, the original Old Absinthe House Bar,
marble-topped and time-worn by the old water dripper (a
sight in itself), is on display at the second location at
Bourbon and Conti streets, an epitaph to Mr. Cazebonne's
ingenuity.

Which brings us to the Café Lafitte in Exile. Again, a
tourist is likely to be confused. At one corner, 901 Bourbon Street, is Café Lafitte in Exile. At the next corner,
941 Bourbon, is Lafitte's Blacksmith Shop, originally known
as Café Lafitte. The "exile" came about like this:

The building housing the original café dates back to
1772 and is historically supposed to have been a blacksmith shop used as a blind by the pirate brothers Pierre
and Jean Lafitte. By 1944 the building had deteriorated.
A "For Sale" sign hung on it. Tom Caplinger, an eccentric
citizen of the world, happened to be honeymooning with
his fourth wife in New Orleans at that time and fell in
love with the building. The price was a mere $5,500, and
Caplinger forthwith plunked down a 10 percent deposit
to obtain occupancy. He immediately opened a bar.
Caplinger had the gift of knowing how to attract customers. Within a year, without so much as dusting cobwebs
from a beam—in order not to destroy the "atmosphere"
— he had, by the sheer force of his personality and his
unlimited stock of outrageous anecdotes, catapulted his
bar into a rendezvous for writers, newspapermen, artists,
entertainers, and that ever-bored group of socialites who
seek surcease from the daily grind of exchanging pleas-
antries with the same old people. Among Tom's steady
customers were Tennessee Williams, Lucius Beebe, and
William March. (The latter wrote *The Bad Seed* in New

Orleans between nightly visits to the old café. The novel was later adapted into a successful Broadway play and a movie.)

But alas, though his bar was crowded night after night, Tom's gullibility and generosity proved to be his undoing. Tom insisted that his friends were always his guests, and their unpaid charge accounts led inevitably to his insolvency. Moreover, he was never able to obtain a clear title to the building, which, he learned had been bequeathed and re-bequeathed to fourteen heirs scattered at various points of the compass. Eventually a court decreed that the executors of the estate could hold a public auction to establish title. The day of the auction Tom and his variegated clientele, many of whom had never risen before noon, were on hand at that hour to witness the proceedings. They had turned out in a holiday mood; the word was that Tom's friends had somehow mustered forty thousand dollars to assure that the building would remain in his possession. But their levity turned to gloom when the bidding went up, up, up, until a rival bar owner bought the place for $42,400, an astronomical figure which Caplinger and his cohorts could not match.

It was the beginning of the end of Caplinger's will to live. But his sense of humor never deserted him. A week later, having vacated the premises, he opened a bar at the next corner and called it Café Lafitte in Exile. He launched it with a "displaced persons" party to which a New Orleans oil heiress wore a burlap sack. But Tom never got over the fact that his new spot was in exile. He had never removed a life-size reclining statue of Adam and Eve that his artist friend Enrique Alferez had sculpted and laid beneath the huge fig tree of the patio of the old café. And when the new owners tore out the bar that Tom had shaped in a serpentine arrangement to simulate the Mis-

sissippi River, it was more than he could stand. He died
in Exile of a broken heart one morning in 1956—the
porter found his prostrate body when he opened up.

Lafitte's Blacksmith Shop, the old café, remains an
interesting bar to visit, but it is no longer the mecca it
once was for celebrities and those who today are called
"the beautiful people." Café Lafitte in Exile, under new
ownership, has become a center for the young "gay" set.
It does a thriving business.

New Orleans also has a haunted house in the French
Quarter, of course, at 1140 Royal Street. The story,
although never documented, is hair-raising enough to
intrigue ghost-lovers. The legend is that the house, a
three-story structure of cement-covered brick, is haunted
by the cries of tortured slaves. The building dates back to
1832, when it was allegedly completed for Dr. Louis
Lalaurie and his family. Madame Lalaurie gained a reputation as a gracious, witty hostess. Her home soon became
a mecca for New Orleans society, and her lavish parties
during the gay Carnival season were the talk of the town.

Then, on the night of May 10, 1834, a fire broke out in
the Lalaurie mansion. It gained headway so rapidly that
neighbors rushed to help extinguish the flames. What
they stumbled upon seared their sensibilities: seven slaves
suffering from varying degrees of starvation and abuse
were wearing iron collars with sharp edges around their
necks, and were chained to the walls of a torture chamber
in the rear of the home. As word of the brutality spread,
outraged citizens rushed into action. Mobs attacked the
premises, rescued the slaves, and carried them off to the
Place d'Armes for public exhibition. In the confusion,
Madame Lalaurie and her husband escaped in their car-
riage. It is thought that they made their way across Lake
Pontchartrain to Mandeville and from there to Paris.

The "haunted" house has recently been restored to its
old exterior elegance. The interior has been converted

into luxury apartments. Meanwhile, tourist guides continue to regale visitors with tales of Madame Lalaurie's
sadistic orgies, embellished with the declaration that on
rainy or foggy nights hoarse voices and the eerie sounds
of clanking chains float out into the midnight air from
the servants' quarters.

Still another fascinating legend—perhaps the most
fascinating—concerns the LePrete mansion at 716 Dauphine Street. It is often referred to as the House of the
Turk. The story is told by Helen Pitkin Schertz, in her
*Legends of Louisiana,* that in the year 1792 the brother of a
Turkish sultan absconded with five wives and much gold
from the sultan's palace. He hired a Turkish freighter,
the *Youseff Bey,* and its crew, and fled the country. Arriving
in New Orleans, he was fortunate to find a suitable
refuge. Jean Baptiste LePrete, an influential banker and
wealthy planter from nearby Plaquemines Parish, was
about to vacate his palatial city home for his plantation
down the river. Arrangements were made for the visiting
royal personage to occupy it during the summer.

Soon the LePrete mansion became known as the House
of the Turk. The sultan's brother entertained lavishly; his
parties became the center of the city's social life. Then
one morning no sound was heard in the house. Eventually the neighbors summoned enough courage to enter.
They discovered the sultan's brother dead in a pool of
blood with the five murdered beauties of the harem
around him. The servants and the crew of the *Youseff Bey*
had disappeared. The explanation, given later, was that
the crew ill at ease and fearing the vengeance of the
sultan's wrath, had murdered their benefactor, stolen his
stolen goods, and sailed to sea as pirates.

This is a good story, but it has a discrepancy. Mrs.
Schertz dates her legend to 1792. The bronze plaque on
the LePrete mansion, visible today, reads "Erected in
1833." But the house is still worth a glimpse if you have

the time. It is a handsome four-story structure with balconies featuring iron grillwork overlooking both Dauphine Street and Orleans Avenue. It, too, is now an apartment house.

Ever hear of a skyscraper only four stories high? There's one in New Orleans at Royal and St. Peter streets. It got its name in 1811 when a third story and a new roof were added to boost a building originally designed to be a story and a half tall. People predicted disaster because the soft soil would not support the added weight. Around 1876, a fourth story was added. It is said the famous New Orleans author George Washington Cable, who established the Creoles in American literature, created his character Sieur George in a unique oval-shaped room on the third floor. Bet you didn't know New Orleans has an Oval Room as does the White House.

New Orleans natives, with their respect for tradition, have a singular reverence for the dead, indeed, almost make a cult of it—they still hold wakes. A wake is a vigil held the night before a funeral. Friends and relatives gather to pay their respects to the bereaved family who sit in the room with the coffin and repeat over and over the circumstances of the death of the departed one. The mourners visit with acquaintances, exchange gossip, and sometimes slip into a festive mood. Coffee is served in a back room of the funeral home. Formerly, cold cuts were also available but, what with inflation, this practice has been discontinued.

A newspaper death notice at the time of the funeral does not always suffice. Many families make it a practice to re-insert an ad on each anniversary of the deceased person's death. Some even compose a rhyme and accompany it with a picture of the departed loved one. Birthdays are also remembered in absentia. Although one's distant cousin may have gone to her reward twenty years ago, it's not uncommon for some member of the family to remind you, "Poor Sophie would have been ninety-three years old today."

But that is nothing compared to the city-wide display of grief on All Saints' Day, November 1, when Orleanians make a public manifestation of their bereavement. I understand this is a Creole custom of European origin unique in the United States. At any rate, November 1 in New Orleans is a city holiday. And no family worth its salt fails to make a pilgrimage to the cemetery to place a bouquet or wreath of flowers on its ancestral tomb. Thus all day long mourners are conveyed by buses and private automobiles to the city's cemeteries—more than thirty of them. There they decorate the graves, kneel and say a little prayer, and take the opportunity to visit with families whose dead lie in nearby tombs.

Burial in tombs is the practice in New Orleans. In the early days the ground was too soggy to bury the dead "six feet under." The grave filled with water before the coffin could be lowered into it. Today, although better drainage facilities make it possible to inter in the earth, it's still the custom to bury above ground. Many of the tombs suggest narrow residences with eaves or rounded roofs. They border paths of narrow asphalt or shelled streets, which bear names like those of a little city. It is this arrangement that gives rise to the description of New Orleans cemeteries as "cities of the dead."

Some of the cemetery architecture is ornate. In Metairie and Greenwood cemeteries there are granite or marble tombs which resemble houses in the French Quarter or Garden District. Some of them have Greek Revival pillars and elaborate cornice work. Sculpture is plentiful—statuary angels, pyramids, obelisks, figures of seraphs in bas-relief, caskets. One tomb contains a vestibule with a stained-glass window of the madonna and child. Some of the large mausoleums are said to cost as much as a hundred thousand dollars. Epitaphs are scarce—the tombs house generations, and the number of names on the marble slabs leaves little space for any expression of sentiment. In addition to tombs there are plain vaults in long neat rows, which Orleanians call "ovens." The more impecunious folk use this method of burial.

For sightseeing purposes, tourists will be interested mainly in Metairie Cemetery for beauty, and St. Louis Cemeteries No. 1 and No. 2 for history. The Metairie Cemetery is located at the intersection of Pontchartrain Boulevard and Metairie Road on what used to be the Metairie racetrack. There's an apocryphal story that a gentleman who was refused admittance to the track's private club later bought the track in a vengeful mood. If *he* couldn't get in, he reasoned, only the dead *could*. Ergo, a cemetery. The St. Louis Cemeteries are near the mid-town section and the Quarter, within walking distance of the major hotels.

A word of caution, however, is in order. Lately, muggers have been frequenting the cemeteries—especially after dark—and tourists are advised not to go into them alone.

To refresh my memory of the annual observance of All Saints Day, I journeyed to these graveyards on a recent November 1. It is an experience that brings one in touch with eternity. Among the mourners were elderly men and women whose remaining years appeared numbered; middle-aged husbands and wives, themselves now parents of children, realizing perhaps too late the love and sacrifices made in their behalf by their own mothers and fathers; and children of the third, fourth, and fifth generations, too young to know the meaning of death, scrambling over the well-kept graves in a picnic mood, begging their parents for ice cream or peanuts from the vendors who inevitably appear wherever crowds gather.

Amidst the profusion of flowers and mourners there were, alas, some weather-stained graves, abandoned except for a lizard or two. One such tomb was encircled by a rusty iron rail and overgrown with weeds. I wondered what had become of the children who had, in tender devotion, placed here the marble urns bearing the words "Mother" and "Father"—urns now full of stagnant water.

Veneration of the dead was evident on many tombstones I stopped to read. They bore a great number of names on the stone tablets and listed life-spans. The notation "Born in France, Died in New Orleans" was not uncommon. In Metairie Cemetery I also brushed elbows with history. To the right of the entrance stands a statue of the Confederate General Albert Sidney Johnston of the Army of Tennessee, who fell at the Battle of Shiloh on April 6, 1862. His is one of the few tombs with an epitaph, part of which reads, "In His Honor, Impregnable: In His Simplicity, Divine." In the mausoleum beneath the towering statue of the general on horseback are buried other soldiers of the Army of Tennessee, among them General P. G. T. Beauregard of New Orleans. General Thomas J. "Stonewall" Jackson of Confederate fame is also commemorated in Metairie. From a handsome granite shaft thirty-two feet high, General Jackson looks down from the center of a large green mound surrounded by palm trees. Beneath him is a mausoleum containing the bodies of 2,500 men of the Army of Northern Virginia.

Two other tombs in Metairie are worthy of notice because of legends concerning them. One is the lavish Moriarity sepulcher to the left of the cemetery entrance; the other is the tomb allegedly built for Josie Arlington, a famous madam of the old New Orleans red-light district. The Moriarity monument is famous for the four huge female statues that adorn it. The story goes that Mr. Moriarity, following the death of his wife, ordered a sculptor to carve the Four Virtues in her memory. "But

Mr. Moriarity," the artist protested, "there are only three virtues, Faith, Hope and Charity."

"I don't care," was Mr. Moriarity's reply, "I want four."

Four he got. Today Orleanians, in explaining the statues, count them off as "Faith, Hope, Charity, and Mrs. Moriarity."

Josie Arlington's tomb is more difficult to find. Cemetery officials would rather not talk about it. When I asked a caretaker if he could direct me to it, he shrugged in feigned bewilderment and replied, "I never heard of it." Yet a pink marble tomb with torches of flaming stone and a bronze figure of a maiden leaning forward to knock on the door once stood in the extreme right section of the cemetery. Harnett Kane shows it in his book *Queen New Orleans* and describes it as Josie Arlington's tomb. The story, well authenticated by Orleanians who swear they saw it during the 1920s, is that a private road with a tollgate bearing a red light for danger was located nearby. When it flashed, it shone on the pink marble facade of Josie's tomb. Thus red lights followed her to her grave.

In the St. Louis Cemeteries lie the interesting graves of Dominique You, a top henchman of Lafitte the pirate; Paul Morphy, of worldwide chess fame; and Marie Laveau, the mulatto voodoo queen. There are also memorials to yellow fever victims and sailors of the seven seas. Some tombs of the original settlers have now almost sunk out of sight.

There are two graves credited to Marie Laveau, whose voodoo powers wielded such a spell over her devotees eighty or so years ago that some of her more gullible followers believed she could turn men into barking dogs. She peddled good- and bad-luck charms and dispensed powders that would put the *gris-gris* on people. The *gris-gris* was allegedly potent enough to kill an enemy. The doubt as to her final resting place is twofold: for one thing, she remained a mysterious figure to the end; for another there were two Marie Laveaus, mother and daughter. The daughter, however, was a lesser sorceress. Some say the real Marie is buried in a marked grave in St. Louis Cemetery No. 1. The tombstone reads: *Famille VVe Paris née Laveau Ci-Git, Marie Philome Glapion, décédée le ll Juin 1897.*

Others assert that she rests in an unmarked "oven" in St. Louis No. 2, where to this day one finds red cross marks scrawled across the concrete slab no matter how often it is painted over. Devotees still bring gifts of food and money, especially on St. John's Eve (June 23)-"Hoodoo Money" in two- and eleven-cent combinations. The belief is that it will bring good luck to the depositor and bad luck to his enemy. It was to this latter grave I was escorted one All Saints Day by two black teenagers named Jerry and John. A path of footprints, sodden from recent rains, led up to the uninscribed slab on this particular oven. "Yassuh," Jerry and John assured me, "this is the real Voodoo Queen's tomb." They pointed to the red cross marks on the slab. There were three, although the slab had been freshly painted for All Saints Day. "If you scratch a mark and pray," they explained, "Marie will make your dreams come true." I came away thinking of another tradition that makes this lovable old city quaint: an Orleanian may revel in the pleasures of the flesh, but he'll not neglect the spirit.

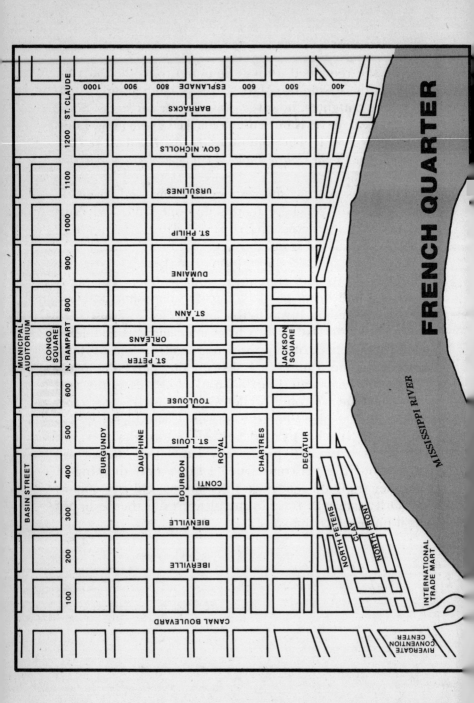

FRENCH QUARTER

MISSISSIPPI RIVER

MUNICIPAL AUDITORIUM

CONGO SQUARE

BASIN STREET

ST. CLAUDE

N. RAMPART

BURGUNDY

DAUPHINE

BOURBON

ROYAL

CHARTRES

DECATUR

NORTH PETERS

CLAY

NORTH FRONT

INTERNATIONAL TRADE MART

RIVERGATE CONVENTION CENTER

BARRACKS

GOV. NICHOLLS

URSULINES

ST. PHILIP

DUMAINE

ST. ANN

ORLEANS

ST. PETER

JACKSON SQUARE

TOULOUSE

ST. LOUIS

CONTI

BIENVILLE

IBERVILLE

CANAL BOULEVARD

1000

900

800 ESPLANADE

600

500

400

1200

1100

1000

900

800

600

500

400

300

200

100

# 3

# The French Quarter

In New Orleans, a saying goes, "The easiest way to get out of the country without leaving the United States is to visit the French Quarter." The witticism has its points: the Quarter's architecture resembles that of the Old World, its food is authentically French Creole, and its Dixieland jazz is about as "far out" as you can get. Moreover, there is a mood—part historic, part romantic, part roguish— that pervades the atmosphere and some of the characters you meet there have no counterpart in this wide, wide world.

The French Quarter comprises ninety or so square blocks in the heart of New Orleans on the north, or downtown, side of the city. It is bounded on the south by Canal Street, on the north by Esplanade Avenue, on the west by Rampart Street, and on the east by the Mississippi River.

On the other hand, progress has taken away the first block fronting on Canal Street by exempting it from the rigid architectural standards imposed on builders for height and design on any new structures in the French Quarter. Several department stores with entrances on Canal Street run through the whole block to Iberville Street, and two new high-rise hotels have been built in the first block.

There is an alternate name for the French Quarter in New Orleans. It is also called the Vieux Carré, meaning old square, because its streets run straight and uniform, in an almost perfect square. They were laid out by a royal French engineer named Adrien de Pauger shortly after New Orleans was founded in 1718.

Its squareness enables tourists to find their way around its confines rather easily if they are following the walking tour maps provided free by the Greater New Orleans Tourist and Convention Commission.

Guided walking tours of the Quarter are also provided by the Jean Lafitte National Historical Park, French Quarter Unit Visitors Center, 916 North Peters Street. The telephone number is 589-2636. After that, if you're not too tired, walking tours are also conducted by the Friends of the Cabildo, starting at the Presbytere on Jackson Square.

You'd also be wise to pick up a little booklet entitled *This Week in New Orleans,* available without charge at most hotel desks. It contains a copy of the walking tour map and a list of events for that week.

Once you enter the Quarter you've crossed the invisible barrier that separates the new city from the old. By daylight it is tranquil. There is a mixed atmosphere of security and adventure in the narrow streets hedged by lacy galleries and the peaceful patios. The old buildings, stained with time, are reassuringly majestic in appearance despite the chips in their once sleek exteriors through which brick ribs are visible. And their preservation is

assured by a city ordinance that prohibits the demolishing
or remodeling of any building without the consent of the
Vieux Carré Commission.

By night the Quarter is naughty, as if darkness releases
the pent-up inhibitions of the day. It is then that tourists,
mesmerized perhaps by candlelight, neon, and the blare
of jazz, let themselves go for a fling. The late actor Paul
Douglas once told me he'd never seen a city do a more
complete flip at sundown.

Bourbon Street, the Quarter's nightlife belt, lined with
bars, nightclubs and restaurants for a distance of almost
nine straight blocks, is of comparatively recent origin. It
burgeoned with a few spots after the repeal of Prohibition, but came into full flower with World War II, when
soldiers, sailors, and marines loaded with pay began to
spill into its confines in droves. One socialite resident of
the area indignantly complained to city officials that she
counted eighty-eight bars and nightclubs in the ninety-
block radius. That was in 1946. Bars never die in New
Orleans, they just multiply. Chances are there are even
more today, but nobody bothers to count.

In other ways the Quarter shows its warm and tolerant
heart. Churchgoers en route to early mass at St. Louis
Cathedral nod politely to sinners on their way to the
French Market for coffee and doughnuts after a night of
revelry. Blacks live at peace next door to whites in a city
that was once determined to fight integration to the last
ditch. Traffic, except at peak hours, has been banned
during certain hours on Royal and Bourbon streets, which
are converted into pedestrian malls. The area around
Jackson Square, the historic part of the Quarter, is now a
permanent mall in which tourists may browse at ease.
Would it surprise you to learn there's not one traffic light
within the Quarter's rigid boundaries? They would mar
the picturesqueness of the area. There are traffic lights

on the fringe streets (Decatur, Esplanade, Rampart, and
Canal) but none within the Quarter proper. Street lights,
to conform to the Old World atmosphere, are of the
ancient gas-lamp type. And mini-buses, designed to resemble little streetcars, roll quietly through the streets.

In this area it's possible to rub elbows with debutantes,
dowagers, drunks, bank presidents, gamblers, actors, collegians, poets, artists, writers, and servicemen. There is
also a typical Quarterite, as distinguished from a typical
Orleanian. He is seldom a native but rather a squatter of
Bohemian propensities. Generally he is a young man with
a yen to write, paint, decorate, compose, or act. He can't
make a livelihood out of his unrecognized talent, so he
takes a job that will provide him with the sordid necessi-
ties of life. He lives in a small apartment, usually garishly
decorated by himself. He dresses slovenly, with a careful
eye to the best effect. He hovers in the St. Peter Street
area, from Jackson Square in the daytime to Bourbon
Street at night. He likes nothing better than to drink and
talk—and pose as "atmosphere" for tourists. This is not to
say the Quarter isn't inspirational to talent. Lafcadio
Hearn, John James Audubon, William Faulkner, Tennessee Williams, Lyle Saxon, Roark Bradford, William March,
Frances Parkinson Keyes, and Gore Vidal have done some
of their best work in its confines.

The Quarter today is being reclaimed in all of its areas.
Industry is moving out. New hotels and motels mushroomed
with such rapidity, the City Council, on request of the
Vieux Carré Commission, placed a ban on further construction of same. However, the majority of them are of
the small luxurious type because of the strict building
regulations; no historic buildings have been lost in the
process. Construction is possible only in cases where sites
are vacant or buildings such as breweries or icehouses
move out. There is a height limit of fifty feet.

For example, the elegant Royal Orleans Hotel was built on the site of the old St. Louis Hotel which had become a surface parking lot after the ancient hotel crumbled from neglect. Only one wall remained on the Chartres Street side and this has been incorporated into the new building whose facade is a reasonable facsimile of the former hotel. Similarly, the Best Western Landmark Hotel on Bourbon Street stands on the site of the old French Opera House which burned in 1919. That site also had

Antique stores line Royal Street in the French Quarter. *(Courtesy Greater New Orleans Tourist & Convention Commission.*

become a surface parking lot. The Royal Sonesta Hotel
replaced a brewery, and the Provincial Motel, an ice
house. Others had to make do by converting only the
interiors of the buildings and restoring the exteriors.

Improvement is still possible in a few sections of the
Quarter but the area has been vastly restored in the last
decade. Real estate prices in the Quarter are at an all-
time high; French Quarter property is the city's most
expensive buy.

On the east, toward the river, Decatur Street is being
steadily upgraded. A few shady bars patronized by seamen
remain. The influx of Cuban refugees has also spawned a
couple of bars which cater to the Latin trade. How about
a bar named the Athenian Room especially for Greek
seamen? There's one on Decatur Street.

The buildings themselves are excellent examples of
tasteful and functional architecture, neither typically French
nor Spanish, but ingeniously adapted to the climate and
topography of New Orleans. Their plain front walls,
right at the property line, form a rampart against the
dust, noise, and crowds of the streets. Their windowless
side walls are a screen against the eyes of neighbors.
From the street, their beauty lies in their iron-lace balconies and perhaps a wrought-iron gate guarding a carriage-
way which leads into a garden courtyard. It is the courtyard, or patio, which the Creoles loved—a cool, secluded
retreat that gave light, privacy, and ventilation to their
homes. Today many of these courtyards, reclaimed in
recent years, contain private swimming pools safely hidden from the street.

Some of the cement-covered brick buildings have been
standing for a century and a half. Many have been
converted into nightclubs, bars, and restaurants. Others
are now antique, curio, art, or perfume shops. Many have
been turned into apartments and rooming houses. A few

Entrance to Jackson Square, known as Plaza d' Armas
during colonial times under the Spanish. Ceremonies
concluding the Louisiana Purchase were conducted here.
St. Louis Cathedral towers in the background. *(Courtesy
Louisiana Office of Tourism)*

Monument to Andrew Jackson, the hero of the Battle of
New Orleans in 1815, in the center of Jackson Square.

still belong to descendants of the original owners. Behind
their facades lie history, romance, and legend. The
walking-tour maps in the free booklets carry a brief
description of many of them if you care to take the time
to meander through the narrow streets. But there are
some sights that rate as "musts" on your visit, and one of
these is Jackson Square, bounded by St. Peter, Chartres,
St. Ann, and Decatur Streets. Here the Quarter's age is

most apparent and inspiring. It was at this spot, on December 20, 1803, that the biggest real estate bargain in history was consummated when the United States took possession of the Louisiana Territory from France.

The square was then known as the Place d'Armes. The name was later changed to Jackson Square in honor of General Andrew Jackson, hero of the Battle of New Orleans fought on January 8, 1815, during the War of 1812. In the center of the square stands a handsome bronze statue to Jackson's memory. The general is shown astride his horse—together they weigh more than ten tons. But the inscription in the base of the monument, *The Union Must and Shall Be Preserved,* has nothing to do with the Battle of New Orleans. It is a garbled quotation of a remark once made by Andrew Jackson which was cut by order of the hated Yankee General Benjamin F. Butler, better known to Orleanians as "Beast" Butler, when he occupied the city during the Civil War.

President Dwight D. Eisenhower added further history to Jackson Square by visiting it and making a speech in 1953, the year of the sesquicentennial celebration of the Louisiana Purchase; the scene of the lowering of the French tricolor and the raising of the Stars and Strips was reenacted for the occasion. General Charles de Gaulle, president of France, visited the square in 1960; and another president of France, Giscard d'Estaing, was also honored on that site in 1976 during his Bicentennial visit to the United States.

Most recently, His Holiness, Pope John Paul II, visited the square and St. Louis Cathedral on September 12, 1987, and dedicated one block of Chartres Street between the square and the cathedral as "Pope John Paul II Place."

The best view of the square is from the Decatur Street entrance with your back toward the river. From this vantage point you get a panorama of the whole ancient architectural setting, with Jackson's statue silhouetted against the facade and spires of St. Louis Cathedral. The cathedral, opposite the square on the Chartres Street side, has become the city's most famous landmark. A picture or painting of New Orleans, or even a poster, is not complete without some part of the cathedral being shown. The cathedral and the square are the mecca for the local artists' colony. Day in and day out they ply their trade along the fences surrounding the square or in Cathedral Alley—known also as Pirates Alley—beside the historic church. They are a colorful, entertaining lot. You can buy one of their typical French Quarter paintings or watercolors for a few dollars or sit and pose for your portrait.

The present cathedral, built in 1794, is the third to occupy the site. The first was destroyed by a hurricane in 1723 the second by a fire on Good Friday in 1788. The fire gained uncontrollable headway because the cathedral

St. Louis Cathedral, flanked by the Cabildo (left) and the Presbytere, on Jackson Square. *(Courtesy Louisiana Office of Tourism)*

bells which ordinarily would have been rung to give the alarm, were stilled because it was thought improper to ring them on Good Friday. The edifice you see today is substantially the same church that was constructed in 1794.

Built of brick and covered with stucco to preserve the mortar from dampness, it followed the pattern of Spanish and South American churches of the period. The facade was flanked by a tower at each extremity, which served as combined watchtowers and belfries, and the intervening roof line was screened by a classic balustrade. The only difference is that a lofty central tower, half again as high as the roof of the church was added thirty years later to

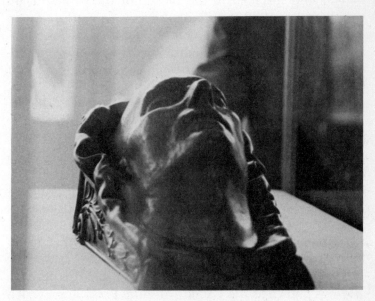

Death mask of Napoleon, donated to the city by the emperor's personal physician. Housed in the Cabildo, this bronze mask is said to be one of only three made from the original mold. *(Courtesy Louisiana Office of Tourism)*

offset the curious emptiness in the middle. This tower
dominates the skyline and makes the structure conform
more to the pattern of European churches.

The outstanding decoration of the interior of the church
is the semicircular painting covering the wall above and
behind the main altar. It portrays the famous incident in
the life of the cathedral's patron saint, Louis IX of
France, when he proclaimed the Seventh Crusade from
the steps of another great cathedral, Notre Dame in
Paris. In the chancel arch a stylized figure of a pelican
symbolizes, by happy coincidence, both Christ and the
state of Louisiana. Six new stained-glass windows depicting
scenes of the Spanish occupation of New Orleans were
donated and installed in the facade of the cathedral on
December 14, 1962, a gift of the government of Spain
through her consul general in New Orleans, Jose Luis
Aparicio. The entire Cathedral has a new-old look because of extensive renovation completed in 1976 at a cost
of $1 million.

In addition, the Washington Artillery Park opposite the
square across Decatur Street has been landscaped, a fountain installed, and an elevated walkway constructed to
provide a view of the Mississippi River on the Moon
Walk. The Walk, built with materials comparable to waterfront use, was constructed in 1976 during the administration of Mayor Moon Landrieu, after whom it takes its
name. It extends one block from St. Peter Street to St.
Ann Street, and there are plans to extend further to St.
Philip Street.

Flanking the cathedral on both sides are two historic
buildings known as the Cabildo and the Presbytere, which
are administered by the Louisiana State Museum. The
Cabildo is the best-known relic of the Spanish domination
of New Orleans. It was built in 1795 to house the Spanish
administrative body and was originally referred to as a
courthouse.

The *Pioneer,* first iron submarine ever constructed, is permanently housed in the Presbytere colonnade. The Confederate navy launched the vessel in 1861. *(Courtesy Louisiana Office of Tourism)*

Constructed of cement-covered brick, the Cabildo is one of the best examples of Hispano-Moresque architecture to be found in the city. In a large room on the second floor, the formal signing of the papers that transferred the Louisiana Territory from France to the United States took place. Among the notables who have been received here are Lafayette, who visited New Orleans in 1825. Others were Henry Clay, Sarah Bernhardt, the Grand Duke Alexis of Russia, Mark Twain, Teddy Roosevelt, William McKinley, General de Gaulle, Dwight Eisenhower, and Valery Giscard d'Estaing—each of whom visited the Cabildo in his own time.

Today the Cabildo houses the main exhibits of the Louisiana State Museum. The Louisiana Transfer Room has been rearranged as an art gallery. One of the most interesting exhibits there is the famous death mask of Napoleon Bonaparte, donated to the city by the emperor's personal physician, Dr. Francois Antommarchi, in 1834. The mold of Napoleon's head was made by the doctor forty hours after Napoleon's death in 1821. The bronze mask on display in the Cabildo is said to be one of three replicas made of the original.

Other exhibits in the building display each period in its history—French Colonial, Spanish Colonial, and American. During the early American period (1803—1853), the Cabildo was used as the City Hall. The Mayor's Parlor and Office are furnished in the American Empire style of the late 1820s. The third floor, added in 1847, includes exhibitions of the Mississippi River, steamboats, and plantation life.

On the opposite side of the Cathedral stands a similar building called the Presbytere. It was begun in 1791, originally intended to be a priests' house. However, it was not until 1813, ten years after the Louisiana Purchase, that the second story was added; in 1847, the third-floor attic and mansard roof completed the building as it stands today. And instead of a priests' house it served as a courthouse until acquired by the Louisiana State Museum. In the Presbytere galleries one may see many aspects of days gone by in exhibitions drawn from the extensive museum collection of original historic material. Portraits and paintings from Louisiana's past, the pageantry of Mardi Gras, antique toys, nineteenth-century firefighting equipment, and 150 years of fashion in Louisiana are highlights of the exhibitions.

Before entering the building, however, turn to the extreme right of the colonnade and you will see the first iron submarine ever built, a creation of the Confederate navy. Constructed in a shipyard on Bayou St. John, the sub was christened the *Pioneer* and launched in the fall of 1861. A tiny craft, it measures only nineteen feet, four inches, in length, and is only six feet high from the keel to the top of the manhole. A crew of four operated it by means of a crank connected with a shaft. Its top speed was four miles an hour. A pair of fins was its submerging apparatus. The *Pioneer* never actually saw war service. It had made only a successful trial run before New Orleans surrendered to federal troops, whereupon the sub was sunk in Lake Pontchartrain to keep the Yankees from capturing it. It was resurrected some years ago as a museum piece and is now interesting as a forerunner of our atomic submarines.

On both sides of Jackson Square are two long, twin, red-brick buildings, of four stories each, with some of the finest cast-iron work in the city gracing their block-long balconies. Known as the Pontalba Apartments, they take their name from the Baroness Pontalba, only child of the wealthy Spanish philanthropist, Don Andres Almonester y Roxas. The baroness had married a cousin and moved to Europe, but the union ended in divorce. In 1848 when she returned to New Orleans, she had architect James Gallier, Sr., draw up blueprints for the buildings. They were completed in two years and are believed to have been the first apartment houses in the United States. Their notable tenants have included Jenny Lind and William Faulkner. Today they are much in demand as good addresses by status-seekers.

Designed in the Renaissance tradition, the apartments have a harmony of proportion restful to the eye. The building on St. Peter Street is administered by the City of New Orleans, and is called the "Upper Pontalba Building." The building on St. Ann Street, under the jurisdic-

Madame John's Legacy, 632 Dumaine Street, possibly
the oldest building in the Mississippi Valley. *(Courtesy
Louisiana Office of Tourism)*

tion of the Louisiana State Museum, is called the "Lower
Pontalba Building." The rooms of the dwelling units are
immense. Their ceilings are very high, as are the windows
that open onto the balconies; in fact occupants are able to
use the windows as doorways. The original fireplaces in
the apartments are still in working order.

The Louisiana State Museum properties include the
Cabildo, the Presbytere, Madame John's Legacy, the 1850
House (in the Lower Pontalba Building), the New Orleans
branch of the U.S. Mint, the Old State Arsenal, the
Creole House, and the Jackson House. Five of the
buildings— the Cabildo, the Presbytere, Madame John's
Legacy, the Lower Pontalba Building, and the U.S. Mint—
are National Historic Landmarks. Visiting hours may be
determined by calling the Louisiana State Museum.

The mint was built in 1835 and, at various intervals in

the nineteenth and early twentieth centuries, it produced silver coinage for general circulation. Today those coins, bearing the letter "O" on the tails side, are collectors items. Transferred to the Louisiana State Museum in 1966, the building has undergone extensive restoration in recent years. It presently houses the Research and Genealogy Library, an elaborate Mardi Gras exhibit, and the New Orleans Jazz Club's collection of memorabilia (including Louis Armstrong's first trumpet).

The 1850 House in the Lower Pontalba Building on St. Ann Street is one of the row houses on the block; it has been restored and authentically furnished in mid-Victorian style. Here you may view a typical residence of the 1850s, complete with courtyard, servants' rooms, and a kitchen equipped with cooking utensils of the period. The beds are made, the dining room table is set. On the ground floor of the 1850 House are exhibitions relating to the history of the Pontalba buildings and Jackson Square.

After inspecting the 1850 House, you need only walk to the corner of Decatur Street and you're on the fringe of the old French Market.

The French Market is a prime tourist area that extends for six blocks along the Mississippi River side of the famous French Quarter. The storied market, now renovated, contains five buildings enhanced by landscaped promenades, bright fountains, attractive benches, and old world light standards. The buildings, while retaining their original facades, have been gutted and glossied up to create curio shops, restaurants, bistros, coffee stands, and dessert parlors.

One old tenant, the Café Du Monde coffee stand, remains in its original site and still does land-office business with café au lait and beignets (coffee and doughnuts to you) with early and late hours clientele. Another coffee stand, Café Maison, has replaced the old Morning Call

farther down the street. A farmers' market (vegetables
and fruit) remains under the outdoor sheds at the rear of
the renovated buildings.

Cost of the market's latest redevelopment was a two-
and-a-half million dollar project, a far cry from the
legend that the market's first site was used by Choctaw
Indians for trading with the French. The first building
was erected in 1791 by the Spanish. This was replaced in
1813 by a meat market. Two of the present French
Market buildings, the coffee houses named above, date
back to 1823. Other buildings were erected in 1912 and
restored by the WPA in 1937.

While in the market area, you may want to visit Madame John's Legacy at 632 Dumaine Street. The building
is a plantation-type raised cottage (lower floor of brick,
upper of wood), built in 1726 by Jean Pascal, a sea
captain. It takes its name from one of the Creole stories

The old U.S. Mint is part of the Louisiana State Museum. *(Courtesy Louisiana Office of Tourism)*

of George Washington Cable in which the hero bequeaths the house to a handsome quadroon known as Madame John. The building is part of the Louisiana State Museum. There is some question by local historians whether Madame John's Legacy is the oldest building in the Mississippi Valley, an honor previously given to the Ursuline Convent a few blocks away at 1114 Chartres Street. The contention is that only parts of the original Madame John's Legacy were used when it was reconstructed after the fire of 1778. The fire of 1778 stopped at the street corner—short of the Ursuline Convent as the Ursuline nuns prayed to a statue of Our Lady of Prompt Succor in their chapel. It was considered a small miracle.

The first Ursuline Convent was completed in 1734; there the Ursuline nuns established the first school for girls in the United States, which they occupied for eleven years. In 1745, French army engineers drew plans for the present building which was completed in 1750. The staircase from the original convent was included in the blueprints and is retained.

So are the twelve-inch cypress beams held together by wooden pegs, not nails. This makes the building adaptable to climatic conditions, because cypress, which grows in swamps, contracts and expands with changes in the weather.

The old convent now has a new name—"The Archbishop Antoine Blanc Memorial." Monsignor Earl C. Woods, current chancellor of the Archdiocese of New Orleans, gives this history of the building: "The Archbishop Antoine Blanc Memorial, located at 1112 Chartres Street in New Orleans, contains the oldest building in the entire Mississippi Valley, the Old Ursuline Convent—Archiepiscopal Residence, constructed in 1745 by the French Colonial Army Engineers under mandate of King Louis XV of

France, who also paid for its construction. Of particular
note is the ancient cypress handmade staircase, which was
removed from the deteriorated original convent and installed in the existing one. The old building housed the
first convent in the United States, the first pharmacy, and
the first classrooms for girls of the white settlers of New
Orleans as well as for the daughters of Indians and of
black slaves. It also housed the first orphanage in the
continental United States, the first college for young men
in the Louisiana Territory, the first classrooms for the
public school system in New Orleans, and the Louisiana
State Legislature when New Orleans was the capital. The
building ceased to serve as a convent in 1824, when the
Ursuline Nuns moved to another location in the city.
After 1824 the property was acquired by the Catholic
Bishops and Archbishops and became the residence of

Interior view of Gallier House, restored home of re-
nowned nineteenth-century architect James Gallier, Jr.
The residence is now a museum. *(Courtesy Louisiana
Office of Tourism)*

the archbishops, the chancery office, and repository for the Archdiocesan Archives, which date back to 1720.

"The building has been completely restored by the Catholic Archdiocese of New Orleans, and is now in full operation as an archival research center and as the repository for the church archives. Admission for research purposes is by written authorization of the chancellor. Tours are conducted each week on Wednesday afternoon by the staff. Other tours are conducted by a tour company through special arrangements.

"Attached to the Old Ursuline Convent—Archiepiscopal Residence is its complement, the Ancient Chapel of the Archbishops, erected in 1845. It is now Our Lady of Victory Catholic Church and houses the National Shrine of St. Lazarus of Jerusalem. Serving first as a house of worship for the French and Creoles of New Orleans, it once served as the Holy Trinity Church for the Germans, St. Mary for the downtown Irish, and later St. Mary's Italian Church, the fourth such church for persons of Italian descent. It was restored in 1978 by the Archdiocese of New Orleans, and once again bears the name of the original chapel, Our Lady of Victory. The church has many notable features, including the old cypress and hard pine ceiling as well as the famous stained class window of the Battle of New Orleans, a donation by President Andrew Jackson. The church is open daily on a limited basis as it is not a parish church with a congregation."

If history is still your bag, there are other museums in the French Quarter worth your inspection. Within its confines are the Musée Conti, a historical wax museum, 917 Conti Street; the Pharmaceutical Museum, 514 Chartres Street; the Historic New Orleans Collection 533 Royal Street; the Gallier House, 1132 Royal Street; and the Voodoo Museum at 724 Dumaine Street.

The Musée Conti was opened on March 14, 1964. It

contains 144 authentically costumed figures, all life-size
and startlingly lifelike, depicting almost three centuries of
New Orleans' legendary history. There are thirty period
settings, accurate in every detail, with one extra for
lagniappe—a "Haunted Dungeon" annex containing
twenty-three wax figures in eleven settings, described as
"the movie monsters you have always known and loved."
One admission fee covers both areas. There are nominal
admission fees for adults and children under twelve.

The historic Pharmaceutical Museum was the former
home of Louis Dufilho who in 1816 became the first
licensed pharmacist in the United States. The building,
erected in 1820, contains four floors and an attractive
patio. A sign outside reads: "La Pharmacie Française de
Louis Dufilho." The museum contains a collection of old
pharmacy and medical instruments from various early
drugstores in the city. A jar marked *Leeches* always attracts
attention. There are old Grecian show-globe urns that
used to decorate drugstore windows; patent medicines,
and hand-made cachets of rice-powder wafers, a forerunner of today's plastic capsules, that were used to sweeten
nasty portions of medicine. The museum is city-owned.
There is a nominal admission charge. Visiting hours are 9
A.M. to 4 P.M. Tuesdays through Saturdays.

The Historic New Orleans Collection is an important
collection of material on New Orleans and Louisiana,
housed in a restored mansion built during the Spanish
Colonial period. Here, brilliantly documented through
original pictorial items, is a panorama of the region. It's
possible to see DeSoto's discovery of the Mississippi, John
Law's financial debacle, the growth of Nouvelle Orleans
in colonial times, the Louisiana Purchase, and the Battle
of New Orleans. There are photos and documents of
New Orleans when she was the boomtown on the Mississippi; of her prosperous plantation days; of New Orleans

as an occupied city during the Civil War; of Reconstruction days; and of the gradual rebirth of the ebullient "Crescent City of the South."

There are eleven galleries in the house where you can see changing exhibitions selected from among thousands of pieces. The ground floor gallery is open to the public, free. A separate tour of the premises includes a "hidden house," the former residence of General and Mrs. L. Kemper Williams that has been completely restored with furnishings authentic to the period. Another building next door to the Historic Collection has been converted into a library in which one may browse. Visiting hours are 10 A.M. to 5 P.M. Tuesdays through Saturdays. There are nominal admission charges for tours of the upstairs galleries or hidden house. The last tour starts at 4 P.M.

Gallier House was opened to the public on July 1, 1971, as a house museum restored to the period of 1860—1868. These were the years it was occupied by renowned architect James Gallier, Jr., and his family, until his death in 1868. Gallier built the Italianate townhouse in 1857—1860. He also built the French Opera House which was destroyed by fire in 1919. Today, the Gallier name is synonymous with mid-nineteenth century New Orleans architecture. Two additional buildings have been added to Gallier House. The exterior of the building immediately adjoining Gallier House has been restored and the interior has been renovated to provide museum facilities and a coffee shop which serves complimentary southern desserts at the end of the tour.

Restoration of the second building was completed in 1975. The garden courtyard has been restored as nearly as possible to its original appearance, with pink and red camellias; white, purple, and red hibiscus; and night-blooming jasmine. Visitors can tour the Exhibition Hall and the restored house, view two films on ornamental ironwork and decorative plaster cornices, and receive the complimentary coffee and dessert. The home is open 10 A.M. to 5 P.M. Tuesdays through Saturdays and 1 to 5 P.M. on Sundays. There are nominal admissions for adults and children. The last tour starts at 4:15 P.M.

The historic Hermann-Grima House and courtyard, 820 St. Louis Street, is open to the public. Samuel Hermann came to this country from Germany and became a wealthy commission merchant in New Orleans. He enjoyed social distinction and prosperity. In 1844 the house was purchased by Judge Felix Grima whose family lived there for five generations. The present owner, the Christian Women's Exchange, bought the property in 1924 and began restoration in 1965. The house and grounds interpret an elegant lifestyle during the "Golden Age" in New Orleans from 1830 to 1860. The Hermann-Grima House has guided tours from 10 A.M. to 3:30 P.M. (closed Sundays.) There are regularly scheduled cooking demonstrations.

It is also possible to feast your eyes on a new, unique museum in New Orleans—Ripley's Believe It or Not! It opened at 501 Bourbon Street on September 28, 1986. An incredible collection of the odd and unusual items gathered from around the world by Robert Ripley are on exhibit. There are hundreds of one-of-a-kind exhibits that shed new light on strange places, strange customs, strange laws, strange hobbies, and strange people. Doors open at 10 A.M. and remain open until midnight.

In the Historic Voodoo Museum, 724 Dumaine Street, you'll find gris-gris objects used for spells, a Marie Laveau display, a Hionfo voodoo altar, music and instruments used in rituals, a live snake also used in rituals, and a psychic reader. The museum, open daily from 10 A.M. until midnight, also conducts a daily 1 P.M. tour of St. Louis No. 1 Cemetery, voodoo tombs, and historic sites. There is one night tour at 7 P.M. Saturdays only.

There is, of course, much more to see in the Quarter if you have the time and inclination. Camera bugs frequently have a field day photographing the elaborate iron-lace balconies of the LaBranche House at 700 Royal Street. The balconies feature a quaint design of entwined oak leaves and acorns.

Many buildings located at intersections in the French Quarter now have tablets of Spanish tile imbedded in their facades with notations explaining what names the streets bore when the city was under Spanish domination. These plaques were provided by the Spanish government a couple of decades or so ago to revive memories of the era of Spanish rule in the city.

You shouldn't miss browsing in the antique shops which line Royal Street for nine blocks. Many open onto garden patios. As you walk, look down at some of the flagstone sidewalks; the paving blocks came over as ballast in ships in the early days.

Lovers of belles-lettres may be interested in an old building at 516 Bourbon Street, where Lafcadio Hearn, in a small rented room, toiled tirelessly over the stories *Chita* and *Youma* that made his name immortal in Louisiana literature.

It is not generally known that in a small apartment at 632 St. Peter Street, Tennessee Williams wrote one of his greatest plays, *A Streetcar Named Desire,* as the Desire streetcar clanged noisily up Royal Street, a few feet from his typewriter. The streetcar has since been replaced by a bus.

The best time for a cultural tour of the Quarter is during the annual Spring Fiesta that is customarily held shortly after Easter. Private clubrooms and homes, ordinarily closed to visitors, are opened to tour groups during this period. Hostesses costumed in antebellum gowns welcome visitors at all stops. A gala "Night in Old New

Orleans" parade, featuring ancient vehicles bearing passengers masquerading as prominent figures of Louisiana
history, passes in review to the tune of marching bands.
And overhead on the iron-lace balconies women singers
impersonate Adelina Patti and Jenny Lind, both of whom
made their mark in New Orleans during residence here.

Information regarding the Spring Fiesta may be obtained
from Spring Fiesta Headquarters, 826 St. Ann Street.
Tours include historic homes and patios in the Quarter
and antebellum homes in the Garden District. There are
also tours of plantation homes in the countryside, night
tours of patios by candlelight, and an outdoor art show in
Pirates Alley. A modest charge is made for the tours. The
art show is free.

Any time of the year, except possibly July or August, is
a good time to visit the Quarter. Walking tours during
those two months may prove uncomfortable because of
the heat. But you'll become as adept as the natives at
ducking into shops, restaurants, or bars for air-conditioned
relief, for New Orleans in summer is almost an entirely
air-conditioned city. Even if you're in town only between
planes, trains, or ships, you'll dine in the Quarter, of
course. But that's the subject of another chapter.

Horse and buggy French Quarter sightseeing tour.
*(Courtesy Louisiana Office of Tourism)*

# 4
# The City Beyond
# the Square

Cross Canal Street from the French Quarter and you're in what we call the American section. It's a part of the city tourists seldom see. But once they enter, most are surprised at the modern contrast to the Vieux Carré. Robert Mitchum, the actor, once was asked to make a personal appearance at a movie theater on the uptown side of Canal Street. He opened his remarks to the audience by saying: "I'm happy to be on this side of the city. I've never been out of the French Quarter before. A friend had told me there was nothing on the other side." Yet the American section is the lifeblood of the city's commerce. Here stand the tall buildings, the banks, and the brokerage houses that make New Orleans a financial center of international trade. Here, too, is the multi-million-dollar Superdome, an all-purpose building for sports, conventions, and theatrical events unmatched in the world to date.

This area was also the site of the 1984 World's Fair

(officially named the Louisiana World Exposition, Inc.). The fair was held from May 12 to November 11, 1984, on an eighty-two-acre riverfront site bounded by Poydras, South Front, Erato, and the Mississippi River. The site included parts of the warehouse district, including Fulton Street and part of South Peters.

The fair's theme was "The World of Rivers—Fresh Water as a Source of Life." This was appropriate because the Mississippi is one of the great rivers of the world. The city tried hard to please visitors to the expo with a monorail for free transportation around the grounds, a separate gondola system for patrons to be airborne across the river from the West Bank, a Wonderwall 2,300 feet long as an ornate midway, and a spectacular Aquacade of pretty girls in bathing suits diving and dancing into the water along with handsome male divers. But, despite these efforts, the fair became awash in red ink. Attendance fell four or five million people below its optimistic projections. It was an artistic triumph, but a financial flop.

However, all was not lost. A major portion of the exposition's former international building is now occupied by the Riverwalk, a commercial enterprise of nationally-famous James W. Rouse under the name "Rouse-New Orleans, Inc." The Riverwalk is a marketplace collection of fashionable clothes, rare gifts, specialty foods, crafted goods, and theme merchandise.

Another boon coming as a result of the fair was several buildings in the warehouse district that were renovated for the occasion are now being turned into condominiums. Also, what had been the fair's huge, flexible Exhibition Hall became the New Orleans Convention Center. The Convention Center offers 381,000 square feet of exhibit space, 100,000 square feet of meeting rooms, a 53,000 square-foot lobby, and a 30,487 square-foot ballroom. Plans are also in the works to expand the facility and create an additional 681,000 square feet of exhibit space on one level.

Another unique building, the Rivergate, constructed at a cost of thirteen and a half million dollars, is primarily a convention center operated by the Board of Commissioners of the Port of New Orleans (which New Orleanians call the "Dock Board"). The building is located at No. 4 Canal Street, near the riverfront. Its main hall has 132,500 square feet of usable floor space to accommodate mammoth trade shows. The design is modern. Every turn of the eye is treated to a new contrast of curves. The ground level seats seventeen thousand people. The huge kitchen can serve ten thousand banqueteers.

The Rivergate, however, is "small potatoes" compared to the Superdome. The Superdome is convertible into an arena for conventions, football, basketball, baseball, and entertainment.

It is so constructed that for standard football competition the capacity is 72,675; for expanded football, 76,791; for baseball, 63,524; and for basketball, 20,000 plus. But, during the "Final Four" extravaganza of the NCAA Basketball Tournament in 1987, the Dome seated 64,959 screaming fans, a new record for that sport. The largest single attendance figure for the Superdome was set in December 1981 when 87,500 rock fans crowded in for a concert by Mick Jagger and the Rolling Stones. However, even that record may be broken in the near future. The Republican National Convention is set to be held there in August 1988, drawing delegates from all over the U.S. and its outlying territories.

The Superdome bore witness to a historical event on September 12, 1987 when Pope John Paul II addressed 45,110 predominately young people during his three-day pilgrimage to New Orleans. Apparently, his blessings were still in the air the following day when the New

Orleans Saints opened their 1987 football season against the Cleveland Browns. In a major upset, the Saints crushed the defending AFC Central Division champs—one of only a handful of times in the team's 20-year history their season began with a perfect record.

The various configurations in the Superdome are made possible by the use of movable stands. Some are mounted on rails and actually roll into place. Others can be put up and taken down when necessary. For conventions, the area provides 470,000 square feet of prime exhibition space.

The Superdome rises 273 feet into the city's skyline. No other building on earth spans the Superdome's 680 feet diameter. The stadium's grounds cover 13 acres. It's the world's largest room unobstructed by posts. It requires 9,000 tons of air conditioning and heating for the Superdome to maintain a temperature of 72 degrees year round.

The Louisiana Superdome, home of the New Orleans Saints. (*Courtesy Louisiana Office of Tourism*)

Major new hotels have been attracted to New Orleans in last several years by construction of the Superdome and nearby office buildings. The latest count on hotel rooms in the greater New Orleans area was 26,000. The Marriott chain opened a hotel 41 stories-high above Canal Street on the edge of the French Quarter. The Doubletree Hotel is adjacent to the Rivergate. A New Orleans Hyatt Regency is next to the Superdome. A New Orleans Hilton is part of the Rivercenter Complex and the Cruise Ship Terminal. Other new hotels in the Central Business District are a large-scale Sheraton Hotel (1,700 rooms); The Inter-Continental Hotel (400 rooms); the Meridien Hotel (508 rooms); the Radisson Suite Hotel (253 rooms); and the Windsor Court (300 rooms).

Presently the tallest building in New Orleans is the fifty-one-story One Shell Square which occupies a whole

Elephants at the Audubon Zoo. (*Courtesy Louisiana Office of Tourism*)

block bounded by Carondelet, Poydras, St. Charles, and
Perdido streets. It towers 697 feet high and has a connecting
parking facility for 750 cars. Its construction was under-
taken by Gerald D. Hines, a Houston investment builder,
who holds other real estate interests in New Orleans.
Because of its shape, many New Orleanians call it "One
Square Shell."

Sightseeing in the American section should begin at
Canal Street. Look up at the lights on the tall standards.
You'll note they're designed to conform to the fleur-de-lis
of France. Study the four bronze plaques embedded in
each base. They'll tell you the flags of the different
governments that have flown over the city in its history.
Specifically they read: "French Domination, 1718—1769;
Spanish Domination, 1769—1803; Confederate Domina-

The St. Charles Avenue streetcar passes the entrance
to Audubon Place. *(Courtesy Greater New Orleans
Tourist & Convention Commission)*

tion, 1861—1865; United States Domination, 1803—1861, and 1865 to date."

I offer two suggestions for a quick grasp of the rest of the city: first, the panoramic view from the observation deck of the World Trade Center on the riverfront; second a harbor tour of the river on one of the riverboats.

Admission to the WTC observation deck, 31 stories high, is nominal. It is open until 10 P.M. Two floors above the deck is the Top of the Mart cocktail lounge from which a panoramic view is also available through plate glass while one sips a drink. The fascination here is that the lounge moves slowly around in a complete 360-degree circumference, so you can drink in the sights while drinking. It takes ninety minutes to make the complete circle. The movement is so slow, three feet per minute, that you aren't aware of motion until eventually you realize you are no longer looking at the river but gazing down the long expanse of Canal Street. One word of caution: don't place any articles on the ledge beside your table if you have a window-view seat. The ledge and windows do not move; the floor and tables do. Women who place their purses on the ledge frequently think they've been robbed when they glance at the ledge and their purses are no longer there. They must chase around the circle for their belongings or take a chance and wait for them to come around again. It adds to the fun of "America's Most Interesting City." Children are not admitted to the Top of the Mart, because food isn't served but alcoholic beverages are. So if you take the kids along for the view, go no higher than the observation deck.

Another panoramic view of the city and river is available from the Top of the Dome restaurant and bar on the thirty-second floor of the Hyatt Regency Hotel, 500 Poydras Plaza. It makes a complete revolution once an hour. It also provides a birds-eye view of the Superdome, for the restaurant is right next door and 87 feet higher than the famous stadium. And children are admitted with their parents to the Top of the Dome because food is served as well as drink.

Cruises on the Mississippi River are discussed more fully in Chapter 1. More than 150 sights of the great port are described by lecturers. Many of the dockside ships fly foreign flags. It's also possible to see U.S. warships ranging from submarines to aircraft carriers because of the Naval Support Actitivies based here. You'll also cruise under the mammoth twin Mississippi River bridges and come close to the old Huey P. Long Bridge. A trolley ride on the St. Charles Avenue streetcar is another way of getting a quick glimpse of the city. The fare is sixty cents each way, with five cents extra for transfers. Express service is also available for 75 cents. Sightseers will witness every architectural style to hit the city in the eighteenth, nineteenth, and early twentieth centuries: great stone mansions; narrow shotgun houses; fine clapboard houses with formal colonnades; turn-of-the-century Victorian whimseys with jutting windows, assorted porches, and stained-glass windows; and, in the last decade or so, too many modern, unadorned, high-rise apartment buildings that offer beehive living in the name of progress. The streetcar winds out of the business district, past the Garden District, through residential neighborhoods, and passes both Tulane and Loyola universities and Audubon Park. The park might make a pleasant stop—there's an interesting zoo in it. (Most Orleanians are friendly and will be happy to point out interesting sights along the way.)

The foregoing will give you an overall picture of the city, but if you can spare the time for a further glimpse of its traditional side, the Garden District is a must for your itinerary. Here the first Americans to arrive in Louisiana

following the Purchase in 1803 settled their own community. Later, during the South's day of glory when cotton
was king prior to the Civil War, they built their handsome
town houses. This was also the era of the river steamboat
when anyone who was anybody came to New Orleans
either as a tourist or a businessman.

The homes built by the newly rich Americans contain
as many as twenty or thirty rooms. A number of them
feature the columns of the Greek Revival period of architecture. Wide galleries or verandahs are much in evidence. A few are built in the typical Louisiana style of the
"raised cottage." Bronze and crystal chandeliers, giant
gilt-edged mirrors, marble fireplaces with matching mantels above, famous murals and statuary, even framed
family trees, add to the quaintness of the spacious rooms
that feature some of the highest ceilings extant in the
United States.

Many of these homes are still in the possession of
descendants of the original owners. Some, however, have
yielded to progress and have been converted into apartment houses or commercial buildings. To stop such ero-
sion, the City Council of New Orleans in 1975 enacted an
ordinance creating an Historic District Landmarks Commission and two historic districts in order to protect the
architectural heritage and environmental quality of older
neighborhoods in the city.

The two districts currently under the jurisdiction of the
Historic Landmarks Commission are the Lower Garden
District and St. Charles Avenue between Jackson Avenue
and Jena Street.

The Lower Garden District lies adjacent to the Mississippi River between the Central Business District and the
Garden District. It contains a viable housing stock of
townhouses row houses, cottages, galleried residences,
churches, commercial buildings, and warehouses of the

19th and 20th centuries. Originally developed in the early 1800s, it was the first semi-urban residential area of New Orleans with large yards and gardens prominent in the area.

The St. Charles Avenue District contains many mansions similar to those found in the Garden District interspersed with others of only slightly lesser architectural interest and many structures important to the scene.

Within the historic districts, the Historic Districts Landmarks Commission will regulate only those outside surfaces of a building that can be viewed from a public street. The commission will regulate ordinary maintenance or those repairs that do not involve a change in the design, material, or outward appearance of a building.

Some historic homes are still preserved. Jefferson Davis, president of the Confederacy, died in a house in the Garden District in 1889. The house, at 1134 First Street, is now privately owned. Then it was owned by Judge Charles Erasmus Fenner, an intimate friend of Davis. Following the war, the Confederate president retired to his plantation home, Beauvoir, in Biloxi, Mississippi, but he was a welcome guest for long periods at Judge Fenner's. There he wrote *The Rise and Fall of the Confederate Government.* In those rooms his beautiful daughter Winnie made her debut. And when, in his declining years, Davis fell ill at Beauvoir, his friends brought him to New Orleans to Judge Fenner's home.

The Louise S. McGehee School, at 2343 Prytania Street, is something to see. Built in 1870, it embodies a wealth of classic detail—fluted Corinthian columns, exquisitely carved exterior and interior woodwork, marble entrance hall and mantels, handsome cornices, eighteen-foot ceilings, and one of the most beautiful spiral staircases in the South.

Several other homes in the Garden District have interesting histories. Among them is the home of George G.

Longue Vue Gardens, a privately owned estate in New
Orleans located within minutes of Canal Street, is one of
the nation's great showplaces. Here one can walk
through a series of five gardens, each with its own plan,
color scheme, and personality. Fourteen fountains,
statues, patios, pebbled walkways, and 100 varieties
of flowers add to the enchantment of this exquisite
estate garden. (*Courtesy Greater New Orleans Tourist &
Convention Commission*)

Westfeldt, Jr., at 2340 Prytania Street. A raised plantation-
type structure built in 1820, the house is reputed to be
the oldest building in the uptown area. It is perhaps
better known as "Toby's Corner," after Thomas Toby,
manager of the Livaudais family who resided there.

At 1313 Eighth Street is the former home of author
George Washington Cable, whose name is associated not
with the Garden District, but with the French Quarter
because Madame John's Legacy, came by its title—a fic-
tional one—from Mr. Cable's novel *Tite Poulette*. The
Cable home, a simple old house built in 1870, features
brick columns, old pivoted windows, and iron gatework.

Gallier Hall on St. Charles Avenue, former city hall.
*(Courtesy Louisiana Office of Tourism)*

On the fringe of the Garden District is an area known as the Irish Channel. In 1976 the National Park Service included the Channel in the National Register of Historic Places. It placed the Channel from Jackson Avenue to Delachaise Street, and from the Mississippi River to Magazine Street. But arguments about the real boundaries of the Channel still persist. The origin of the name is uncertain, although at one time the residents were predominately Irish seafarers and the district was known as one of the tougher spots in New Orleans. The sector has lost most of its individuality today, but there's one landmark worthy of note: the Frances Kaul house at 904 Orange Street.

The house, dating back to the 1830s, was known historically as the Goodrich-Stanley House, the boyhood home of the famed explorer Sir Henry Morton Stanley, who discovered Dr. David Livingstone in darkest Africa on November 10, 1871. Stanley's original name was John Rowlands. He was a native of Denbigh, Wales, but when he came to New Orleans as a youth, he took the name of his adoptive father, Henry Hope Stanley, a cotton merchant, and called himself Henry Morton Stanley. His signature was cut into a glass windowpane of the little room he occupied between the kitchen and the front bedrooms. The house, alas, was sold at auction in January 1981, and moved to a lot on the corner of Coliseum and Polymnia Streets on Coliseum Square. ('Tis hoped the glass windowpane bearing Stanley's inscription is retained.)

On upper St. Charles Avenue, in the 6300- and 6400-blocks, stand Tulane University and Loyola University of the South, side by side. Tulane, the older of the two, resulted from a merger of the Medical College of Louisiana (founded in 1834) and the University of Louisiana (1847). It came by its present name in 1883 when a bequest of a million dollars by Paul Tulane transformed the struggling college into one of the country's finest medical and law schools.

Loyola University is a Roman Catholic institution operated by the Society of Jesus. It was founded in 1911 as an outgrowth of Loyola Academy, a preparatory school that had occupied the site since 1904. The main buildings on the fourteen-acre campus face St. Charles Avenue, grouped around three sides of a square.

Opposite both universities is Audubon Park, a 400-acre plot of ground extending from St. Charles Avenue to the Mississippi River. The grounds are part of the Etienne de Boré estate, upon which sugar was first successfully granulated in 1794. The park, named for John James Audubon, contains a bronze statue to the memory of the famed ornithologist. The statue previously stood half-hidden in a grove of trees. Presently, it's one of the attractions in the park's recently renovated zoo, which has been expanded from 13 to 58 acres, with many new facilities added at a cost of $20 million. Practically every species of animals

City Park in New Orleans. *(Courtesy Louisiana Office of Tourism)*

and birds may be found within its confines. Indeed the Audubon Zoo several years ago had the distinction of preserving one vanishing species of birds. Its two whooping cranes, the late Jo and Crip, attracted national publicity for being the first of their species to become parents in captivity, but there are no longer any whooping cranes at the zoo.

In addition to the zoo, the city has also established a Louisiana Nature and Science Center, dedicated to providing education in the natural sciences and the interdependence of man and nature in Louisiana's unique coastal environment. The center is located in Joe Brown Park in eastern New Orleans, 11000 Lake Forest Boulevard. It is an 86-acre wildlife preserve—a bottomland hardwood forest—packed with the flora and fauna of our state. Hands-on exhibits feature a Discovery Loft, a working beehive, an Education Center with its planetarium, a teaching greenhouse, and an open-air café.

Monument to John McDonogh, philanthropist and benefactor of the New Orleans public schools during the late
nineteenth century.

Dr. Robert A. Thomas, executive director of the Center, says, "Three trails course through the woods making it possible to observe the wetlands and wildlife that abounds. It is particularly nice to enjoy the quiet serenity of the woods while observing the many animals and wildflowers. One is likely to see swamp rabbits, raccoons, turtles, and a variety of birds." For information about hours and admission, call 246-9381.

If you have children, you shouldn't miss the Louisiana Children's Museum, 428 Julia Street, near the former site of the world's fair. It opened its doors on October 11, 1986, and is dedicated to a sharing experience between adults and children by permitting them to put their hands on the exhibits. It is also an exciting educational resource that helps teachers enrich children in the social studies of art, math, language, and science curricula.

Popularity of the Children's Museum is growing so fast that expansion plans are already underway. Presently it is open Tuesday through Sunday, 9:30 A.M.—4:30 P.M. No food or drinks allowed. For further details, call 523-1357. The executive director is Debra Bresler.

Longue Vue Gardens, a privately-owned estate in New Orleans located within minutes of Canal Street just off Metairie Road, is one of the nation's great showplaces. Here one can walk through a series of five gardens, each with its own plan, color scheme, and personality. Fourteen fountains, statues, patios, pebbled walkways, and 100 varieties of flowers add to the enchantment of this exquisite estate garden. For information about tours and hours call 488-5488.

Like other southern cities, New Orleans is proud of her mementos of the Civil War. A statue of General Robert E. Lee gazes north on the top of a sixty-foot shaft of Tennessee marble at the intersection of St. Charles and Howard avenues. Around the corner, at 929 Camp Street, is the

Confederate Museum, which contains many relics of some of the bloodiest battles fought in the Civil War. A statue of Jefferson Davis, president of the Confederacy, stands in a well-kept parkway at 3400 Canal Street. He is portrayed in a standing position, as if speaking to the nation about the convictions he held.

And on Canal Street, near the riverfront, there is a simple granite shaft in the center of the neutral ground dedicated to brave Orleanians who fought a pitched battle to rid the city of carpetbagger rule. They were members of the Crescent White League, a military organization of citizens formed in June 1874, to protect Orleanians from "Negro aggression," as they called it. The skirmish between opposing forces on September 14, 1874, resulted in twenty-one members of the league being killed and nineteen wounded, but it ended in the capitulation of the Yankee-imposed metropolitan police. Descendants and friends of members of the league still gather for ceremonies around the monument every September 14. But in recent years, with the city population now half black, protest developed against the words "white supremacy" inscribed on the statue, As a result, city officials ruled the offending words be cut off the monument.

An equestrian statue of General P. G. T, Beauregard, the "Great Creole" of the Civil War who gave the command to fire the first shot on Fort Sumter, overlooks the Esplanade Avenue entrance to City Park. City Park is well worth a visit. If you're an art lover, here you'll find the New Orleans Museum of Art. Three new wings have been added to the original building, the Isaac Delgado Museum, which is over sixty years old. The new wings, opened to the public on November 21, 1971, are: the Wisner Education Building; the Stern Auditorium; and the City Exhibition Wing, which includes the Ella West Freeman Memorial Gallery and the Felix J. Dreyfous

Memorial Library. The original building retains its name.
One of the portraits of note is that of Estelle Musson of
New Orleans painted by the great French impressionist
Edgar Degas during his visit here. Also on display is part
of twenty-two sections of the Kress collection. There are
outstanding examples of pre-Columbian art, bronzes by
Rodin, canvases by contemporary artists, plus such masters as Picasso, Miro, and Jackson Pollock. And adorning
the exterior of the entrance to the museum is a bronze
statue of Hercules as an archer by Bourdelle. The Museum also played host to the King Tut and Search for
Alexander exhibits during their international visits to the
United States from Egypt and Greece, respectively.

City Park also contains a dueling oak under which
Creoles settled affairs of honor with swords, pistols, or
Bowie knives until one or the other fell in combat.
McDonogh Oak, another famous tree in the park, is
estimated to be in excess of 600 years old. It has a branch
spread of 142 feet. In 1958, when the National Parks and
Recreation Centers Association met in convention in New
Orleans, Ellis Laborde, then City Park Superintendent,
hosted a breakfast for 526 people shaded by the tree.

Students of architecture will be interested in the Custom House on Canal Street, not far from the Liberty
monument of the Crescent White League. The massive
granite building, which occupies the entire block bounded by Canal, Decatur, North Peters and Iberville streets,
was begun in 1847; but what with the Civil War and
various architectural problems, it was 33 years in construction. Now more than 130 years old, the Custom
House was designated a "historic custom-house" as part
of the Customs Bureau's contribution to the U.S. Bicentennial celebration. Local legend had it that the founda-
tions were laid on cotton bales and the cornerstone was
laid by Henry Clay. 'Tisn't so. Its foundation is based on

heavy cypress planking, surmounted by a grillage of twelve-inch logs, topped with a one-foot layer of concrete. And although Henry Clay attended the ceremony on February 22, 1849, the customs collector Denis Prieur, laid the cornerstone.

The highlight of the interior of the building is the Marble Hall the large business room in the center of the Customs Department. Measuring 128 by 84 feet, with a height of fifty-eight feet, it contains panels of life-size bas-reliefs of Bienville and Jackson. The ceiling consists of a white and gold iron frame set with enormous ground-glass plates supported by fourteen columns of pure white marble. The floor, of black and white marble, is set with heavy glass to provide light to the rooms below. As you enter from the comparatively dark corridors, the sunlight-bright hall makes you blink.

So what's New Orleans got to offer in the way of modernity? Well, there's the Civic Center, beginning at Tulane and Loyola Avenues, of which many Orleanians are not proud. The boxlike ungraceful lines of this cluster of public buildings, all windows or unadorned walls, are as cold to the eye as an ice cube. Worst of all is the new public library building, flat-topped and encased in a dark iron screen. It looks like a warehouse on the waterfront. The Civic Center does boast a statue of George Washington, dedicated February 8, 1960, a gift of the Louisiana Grand Lodge of Free and Accepted Masons. It shows the robust father of our country wearing a Masonic apron and jewelled pendant as master of his lodge. He holds a gavel in his right hand.

A statue of John McDonogh—who bequeathed his fortune equally to the public schools of Baltimore, his birthplace, and New Orleans, his adopted home—has been transported to the plaza of the Civic Center from its former resting place at St. Charles Avenue and Toledano

Street. Here, each year on the first Friday in May, the school children of New Orleans make a pilgrimage and pay their respects to their benefactor by laying bouquets of flowers and floral wreaths before his monument. There is another statue of John McDonogh in Lafayette Square. President John F. Kennedy's visit to New Orleans on May 4, 1962—to dedicate a new dock on the riverfront—was on McDonogh Day. When he delivered an address at noon from the balcony of City Hall, he spoke before the flower-banked statue of John McDonogh and a square full of students who had decorated it.

The newest monument in the Civic Center honors deLesseps S. Morrison, the dynamic young New Orleans mayor who served four terms from 1946 to 1961, after which he was appointed U.S. ambassador to the Organization of American States by President Kennedy. He held that post from 1961 to 1963. He was killed in a plane crash in Mexico on May 22, 1964. It was during his mayoral administration that the Civic Center was built. He also built new underpasses and overpasses that speed up traffic hitherto congested by numerous dangerous railroad crossings. The monument to "Chep" was dedicated May 22, 1965, exactly one year after his death, and it was unveiled on January 18, 1971. The sculptor was Lin Emery Braselman of New Orleans. The memorial is a forty-foot metal shaft opposite a reflecting pool. A figure of Morrison faces the pool. The other three sides contain dates and descriptions of the highlights of his political and military careers.

Adjacent to the Civic Center, a little farther up Loyola Avenue, in front of the Union Passenger Railroad and Bus Terminal, stands the statue of Jean Baptiste le Moyne, Sieur de Bienville, founder of New Orleans. The sculptor was Angela Gregory, also of New Orleans.

Other statues—tangible evidence of how New Orleans

rates as a good neighbor to Latin America—are those of
Simon Bolivar, Benito Juarez, and General Francisco
Morazon. Bolivar, of course, freed much of Latin America
from Spain. His twelve-foot statue, a gift to the city from
the people of Venezuela, was dedicated November 24,
1957. It is first in line at Canal and Basin streets,
ornamented by a pool and fountain. Juarez comes next,
further down Basin Street. The statue of Mexico's "Abraham
Lincoln" was given by the people of Mexico and bears the
Juarez quotation: "Peace is based on the respect of the
rights of others." The third Latin American monument,
at Basin and St. Louis streets, is dedicated to General
Francisco Morazon, the hero of Central America. It was
given to us by Honduras, a country with close ties to New
Orleans; the republic of El Salvador also participated in
the gift. The statue was dedicated October 21, 1966.

On the residential side are several subdivisions called
Gentilly, Mirabeau, Lakeview, Lake Vista, Lake Terrace,
Lakewood, and the nearby suburban community of Metairie.
Here you'll find the luxurious rambling ranch houses, the
modern mansions of the sort you see illustrated in *House
Beautiful* and *Better Homes and Gardens*.

For a tourist, a drive along Lake Pontchartrain and its
environs will afford the easiest and quickest way to grasp
this picture. Many costly residences of ultramodern design can be seen from a broad concrete highway, five-and-
a-half miles long, which parallels the lake. During the
warm months another interesting sight is possible. A
parkway adjoining the sea wall, also along the highway,
teems with picnickers and swimmers seeking fun and
surcease from the heat.

It's also possible for vehicular traffic to cross Lake
Pontchartrain on the Lake Pontchartrain Causeway—the
longest bridge in the world at twenty-four miles. It extends from Metairie in Jefferson Parish to Mandeville in

St. Tammany Parish, and there is a one dollar toll each way.

Of course, for a comprehensive tour of the city, touching on all points of interest with bits of information concerning each, a sightseeing bus is recommended. The buses call at all hotels for passengers who have made reservations with the doorman or by telephone. Guides who explain each sight as you go along are well trained and informed. Some even resort to humor en route to keep you entertained. One, for instance, tells his passengers there's a city ordinance which prohibits anyone living within a half mile of historic St. Louis Cemetery No. 1 from being buried in it. When the startled group asks why, he blandly explains, "Because they have to be dead."

Statue of Simon Bolivar, liberator of South America, at the corner of Canal and Basin streets. (*Courtesy Louisiana Office of Tourism*)

# 5

# What to Eat and Drink

Discard your diet when visiting New Orleans. You'll never be able to stick to it. Sauces rich in wines, herbs, and spices are the features of almost every dish served in the better restaurants. No true gourmet would think of having dinner without an aperitif before the appetizer, or the proper wine with the entrée, or an after-dinner liqueur or Café Brûlot as a finale.

Shall we then begin with a cocktail? In New Orleans it's the Sazerac. (You can drink your martinis elsewhere.) The Sazerac is a drink somewhat more potent than the light dry or sweet wine the rule-book suggests, but to visit New Orleans and not try a Sazerac is akin to returning from Rome without having had an audience with the pope. The Sazerac's ingredients are: one cube of sugar dissolved in a teaspoon of plain water, one dash of Angostura bitters, two dashes of Sazerac bitters, one and a quarter ounces of rye whisky. All this is stirred in a glass chilled with ice; a second glass is then rinsed with three dashes of an absinthe substitute (Herbsaint or Pernod), and the contents of the first glass are strained into the second. Finally, the oil of a lemon peel is squeezed over the top. Probably the only famous visitor to New Orleans who "passed" after hearing the play-by-play description was Joan Crawford, but she graciously explained she didn't drink whiskey. She then ordered her customary vodka on the rocks.

For those like Miss Crawford who are non-whiskey drinkers, another popular local concoction is the Ramos gin fizz. This drink was such a favorite of the late, tempestuous Huey Long that he once ordered a Roosevelt Hotel bartender flown up to New York to mix him one when the bartender in his hotel was unable to concoct one to suit the Kingfish's taste. Here is the recipe: one teaspoon powdered sugar, a half-teaspoon of orange-flower water, one jigger of gin (two are better), the juice of half a lemon, the juice of half a lime, one egg white beaten well, half a glass of crushed ice, two teaspoonsful of rich cream, one ounce of seltzer water; shake until tired, then shake again.

Whether you've had a Sazerac or a Ramos fizz, the next step is dinner. You should try seafood—it's the specialty of most of the better restaurants, for the waters surrounding the city abound in fish, crabs, oysters, and shrimp. One of the more popular gastronomic delights is Oysters Rockefeller, a dish so rich that its creator, Jules Alciatore, son of Antoine Alciatore, founder of Antoine's (one of the city's most famous restaurants) could only think to name it after the then-richest man in the world John D. Rockefeller. So you'll have it at Antoine's, 713 St. Louis Street, of course. As nearly as it can be described for the exact recipe is a secret still closely guarded by the third generation of the family—Oysters Rockefeller is prepared as follows: raw oysters on the half shell are

topped by a highly seasoned mixed green dressing and
baked on a bed of ice-cream salt, with the heat applied
from both above and below.

The oysters are the appetizer. For the entrée, try Pompano en Papilotte, a dish created when a famous French
balloonist was to be entertained at Antoine's. To resemble
a balloon, the chef baked a filet of pompano in a waxed
paper bag stuffed with crabmeat and shrimp immersed in
a white wine sauce. The dish has become a specialty of
the house. It should be accompanied by Pommes Soufflés
(blown-up potatoes), which look like the customary French
fries but whose center is nothing but air. A mixed green
salad with French dressing and a Baked Alaska for dessert might round out a typical dinner at Antoine's.

But don't picture Antoine's as being elaborately decorated with gold-, silver-, and bronze-leaf plastered in the
recesses of the ceiling, or expect to hear a select orchestra
softly playing excerpts from operatic arias or see a foot-
man in livery opening a car door. Antoine's is today what
it was at its inception in 1840—an unadorned restaurant
with plain, family tableware and linen and attentive waiters. When you go to Antoine's, it is to give your palate
undisturbed pleasure.

If it's atmosphere as well as cuisine you seek, the place
to go is Brennan's, 417 Royal Street. Brennan's founded
in 1946 by the late Owen Brennan is now managed by his
three sons, Owen, Jr., James, and Theodore. The restaurant is housed in the Patio Royal, built in 1801, once the
site of the Bank of Louisiana and later the residence of
Judge Morphy, father of the international chess king Paul
Morphy. The floor of one of the rooms of the restaurant,
now covered by a wall-to-wall carpet, is laid out in dark
and light mahogany squares to resemble a chess table.
The Brennans have redone the premises in warm and
elegant taste to bring the interior up to date. A view of

the luxuriant tropical patio is provided from any table in the downstairs rooms.

Despite its Irish name, Brennan's features French and Creole food and makes a specialty of a large and leisurely French breakfast. Grilled grapefruit, Creole cream cheese with fresh fruit, and a variety of egg dishes are among choices offered on the menu. My favorite is Eggs Sardou, in which the eggs are poached on artichoke bottoms and topped with creamed spinach and Hollandaise sauce. The eye-opener that precedes breakfast should be an Absinthe Suissesse (one and a half ounces of Herbsaint; the white of an egg; one teaspoon of cream; half a teaspoon of orgeat syrup, and a dash of anisette). And of course you'll have a good rosé wine during the meal.

But breakfast is only one of the attractions of Brennan's. An after-dinner dessert that has gained local popularity is "Bananas Foster." The restaurant is also the birthplace of the famous Mardi Gras Krewe of Bacchus that made its sensational debut of celebrity kings in 1969 with the late Danny Kaye.

Galatoire's, at 209 Bourbon Street, is a small but extremely popular restaurant that many Orleanians contend has the best food in town. It is certainly the most independently operated; for no matter who you are, the management will not take a reservation; nor does Galatoire's advertise. One gets there early enough to get a table (11:30 A.M. for lunch, 6:15 P.M. for dinner) or stands in line outside until one is vacant.

Galatoire's was founded in 1905 by the late Jean Galatoire. It is still operated by members of the family with little or no change in policy. A fire gutted the premises several years ago and caused extensive damage, thus providing an opportunity to redo the dining room—which, with its bright overhead lights and mirror-lined walls, had been

facetiously referred to by Orleanians as a glorified barbershop. But what did the third generation of the founding
family do? They called in a contractor to put everything
back the way it was. There's no deviation from policy,
either. The restaurant closes every Monday, and that goes
for the busy Monday before Mardi Gras (Fat Tuesday), or
the day of the Sugar Bowl game if that falls on a Monday.
I do believe—and many a patron of Galatoire's will back
me up—that the management wouldn't open on a Monday for the President of the United States.

Trout Marguery—trout poached in a highly seasoned
fish stock and served in a rich egg-and-wine sauce—is the
specialty of the house. But Pompano Amandine and
stuffed eggplant (with crabmeat and shrimp) run close
seconds. Many Orleanians swear everything on the menu,
including the drinks, is special.

Several other restaurants in the French Quarter feature
Creole cuisine. Among them are Arnaud's at 813-819
Bienville Street; Broussard's, 819 Conti Street; the Court
of Two Sisters, 613 Royal Street; Vieux Carre, 241 Bourbon Street; and Tujague's, 823 Decatur Street. All of
them have enjoyed a devoted clientele over the years.

Arnaud's restaurant, long a revered name in New
Orleans, dates back to 1918, when it was opened by
Arnaud Cazenave, whose grand manner and joie de vivre
earned him the fictitious title of Count long before Mike
Romanoff became a prince. The Count died on May 30,
1948, and the restaurant was bequeathed to his daughter,
Mrs. Germaine Cazenave Wells, who ran the business
herself until her death in 1983.

After that, Arnaud's was bought by Archie Casbarian, a
former general manager of the posh Royal Sonesta Hotel
in the French Quarter. He retained the restaurant's name
but extensively renovated it, improving its decor and

cuisine. Since its rebirth, Arnaud's has been regaining favor with New Orleanians, always a good criterion of French and Creole food.

The most "atmospheric" restaurant in the French Quarter is the Court of Two Sisters. It runs an entire block, with entrances on both Royal and Bourbon Streets. A huge patio filled with tropical horticulture and a wishing well occupies the center where, weather permitting, food is served. The Court in many ways typifies the old city. The building and grounds, designed by Pierre de Rigaud, Marquis de Vaudreuil, an early governor of territorial Louisiana, were planned to create an atmosphere of la belle France. The restaurant takes its present name from two maiden ladies, Bertha and Emma Camors, who in 1886 opened a shop on the ground floor and called it the Shop of the Two Sisters. The present proprietors are Joe Fein III and Jerry Fein, who inherited the restaurant from their father, Joe Fein, Jr. Appreciation of atmosphere, like taste for food, is a matter of personal preference. The Court offers a variety of Creole and French dishes. The cuisine is not as popular with Orleanians as it is with tourists. For my part, however, I've enjoyed many a good dinner at the Court of Two Sisters.

Broussard's, 819 Conti Street, is another old name among local restaurants which, like a phoenix rising from its ashes after a period of desuetude, was reopened in splendor in 1975 under the proprietorship of Joe Segreto. It is presently one of the most beautiful restaurants in town. Broussard's features three elegantly furnished dining rooms and a bar, all opening to a lush patio. The cuisine is New Orleans Creole, with such dishes as Duck Nouvelle Orleans, Chicken Rochambeau, Oysters Gresham, and Trout Conti to make you drool in anticipation. The present owners are George Huber, Gunter Preuss, and his wife Evelyn Preuss.

Tujague's is unique. It has no menu. One comes in, sits down, and allows the waiter to serve the lunch or dinner of the day. The new proprietor, Steven Latter, bought the restaurant on November 23, 1983, and continues the same practice. "We serve seafood, poultry, and red meat in Creole style," Steven says, but he also admits two of Tujague's longtime popular dishes, Shrimp Remoulade and Brisket of Beef with Horse-Sauce, are always served.

K-Paul's Louisiana Kitchen, 416 Chartres Street, is a small unpretentious restaurant that owes its popularity among New Orleans diners to its renowned chef, Paul Prudhomme, undoubtedly one of the country's masters of Cajun and Creole cuisine.

He learned to cook from his mother in Opelousas, Louisiana; by the time he was 17 he had his own restaurant. Later he traveled around the country, adding to his knowledge of food by picking up odd cooking jobs en route. He moved to New Orleans in 1972 as executive chef at the Maison Dupuy Hotel. After a successful stint there he moved to Commander's Palace, continuing meanwhile to expand his reputation nationally by supervising dinners in Washington, D.C., and New York City.

In 1979 he decided to go into business again, this time with partner Kay Hinrichs, whose initial is affixed to the restaurant's title. (They met when both were working at the Maison Dupuy.) K-Paul's serves Cajun and Creole food; the menu changes daily.

There's also a French restaurant, Maison Pierre, at 430 Dauphine Street, très élégant in every detail. The ornate dining rooms occupy a typical New Orleans cottage built in 1780 which has been beautifully restored. Maison Pierre opened its doors in September 1969 under the supervision of chef-owner Pierre Lacoste, Jr., whose father Pierre Lacoste, Sr., and grandfather Justin Lacoste had preceded him in the business. The restaurant is now in its fourth generation and its staff is wholly in the family. Pierre's wife, Doralyn, operates the business, and three of their four sons and one daughter serve the tables. A fourth son, age 7, opens the door and will play his violin on request only.

Begue's, a name famous in New Orleans's culinary past, was a Creole restaurant in the French Market area. The original is no longer in existence but the name has been given to a handsome new restaurant at 300 Boubon Street in the Royal Sonesta Hotel. The new Begue's opened in September 1969. It's still in the hotel, but has recently been expanded and moved to another area that had been called the Green House. Where the Green House was, is now Begue's; and Begue's has been lavishly redone, enlarged, and raised slightly in height so its patrons will have a view of the hotel's landscaped tropical patio. And the area that had been the first Begue's dining room in the hotel is still there. It has been renovated to accommodate formal receptions or large corporate dinners that had been taking place more frequently in the dining area.

La Louisiane, 725 Iberville Street, a historic institution of fastidious dining for over a hundred years, has been under the management of chef-partner Nick Mosca, Joe Marcello, Jr., and his son, Joe III, since January 1979. The same partners formerly operated the Elmwood Plantation Restaurant, 5400 River Road, which, was gutted by fire on December 18, 1978. That prompted the proprietors to scout around for another location in the city proper. When La Louisiane became available, they took over the lease from the Moran brothers, Jimmy Jr. and Tony.

The famous old restaurant was completely renovated at a cost of half a million dollars and today glows with class in all the appointments of its decor. Special Creole and

Italian dishes of the house include Oysters Mosca, Veal Picata, Trout Lafreniere, Calamari, and Stuffed Veal Chops with Oyster Dressing.

Among the newer restaurants in the French Quarter is Mr. B's Bistro, owned and operated by Dick, Ella, Dottie, and John Brennan, owners of the famed Commander's Palace in the Garden District of New Orleans. Mr. B's location, at 201 Royal Street, on the corner of Iberville Street, happens to be about the busiest hub of pedestrian and motor traffic in the Quarter. And the Brennans have taken advantage of this perspective by placing large plateglass windows around the dining room, which faces both streets to provide patrons with an ongoing parade of people passing in review.

Mr. B's, which opened in September 1979, is reminiscent of oldtime New Orleans restaurants and saloons. The decor is restrained and real, with oak flooring, warm wood paneling, and plain marbletop tables. The sixty-five-foot mahogany bar was custom-made in place. The restaurant serves breakfast (weekends only), lunch, and dinner. Oldtime New Orleans dishes and some new ones that have been created at Mr. Bs—like Shrimp Chippewa and Mr. B's Chocolate Cake—are on the menu. A prominent national food critic termed Mr. B's "one of the most innovative restaurants to open in New Orleans in some time."

Café Sbisa, 1011 Decatur Street, is opposite the French Market. The building dates back to 1827. It was bought in February 1979, by Dr. Larry Hill and John Pico, who renovated the interior from top to bottom. Their experience as restaurateurs dates back to 1971. The café's specialty is bouillabaisse, a concoction of fish and shellfish mixed with piquant ingredients into a sort of soup. Another favorite of patrons is charcoal-broiled redfish. The restaurant is opened for dinner from 6 P.M. to midnight,

Tuesdays through Sundays, and serves a popular Sunday brunch from 11 A.M. to 3 P.M.

Moran's Riverside, at 44 French Market Place in the renovated Market complex, is a handsome new second-story restaurant with a view of the Mississippi River and its waterborne traffic that is the best in town. It also provides a look at French Quarter rooftops on the other side of the dining room. The owner, Jimmy Moran, Jr., offers a menu that features seafood in French and New Orleans Creole style, plus Roman pasta dishes he learned from his mother and father. Jimmy also spent eleven weeks in Italy studying the latest Roman recipes. The pasta dishes—fettucine and cannelloni—are prepared from fresh pasta made on the premises. One of the restaurant's distinguished visitors was King Hussein of Jordan who was entertained here by Mayor Moon Landrieu on April 2, 1976, during a state visit. Jimmy served the king Baby Veal Picanto and fettucine. (The history of the site of Moran's Riverside, opposite the crescent bend of the river, was researched by Sam Wilson, the French Quarter's most noted historian-architect. He blueprinted the present building as nearly as possible to match the original structure.)

Some of the new, smaller luxury hotels in the French Quarter have excellent restaurants in their buildings. The Louis XVI Dining Room of the Marie Antoinette Hotel, 827 Toulouse Street, recently moved into the St. Louis Hotel, 730 Bienville Street. It serves what they describe as "Epicurean European Cuisine." The Maison Dupuy Hotel, 1001 Toulouse Street, has a tempting menu of Cajun-Creole cuisine that's sure to tempt your palate. The Hotel Monteleone runs the gamut from a posh dining room to an oyster bar and seafood restaurant just off the lobby with a fascinating title, The Aft-Deck, to complement its nautical decor.

Variety being the spice of life, not all restaurants in the Quarter are French. There are several good Italian restaurants, as well as two establishments that feature prime ribs. The Italian restaurants are Tortorici's, 441 Royal Street, and Messina's Oyster House, 200 Chartres Street. Featuring prime ribs are the Rib Room of the Royal Orleans Hotel, 621 St. Louis Street, and Robert's Steak House, 111 Iberville Street. The former is a handsome hotel dining room. The latter is composed of three converted railroad cars and a caboose that offers a unique atmosphere. If prime ribs of roast beef are your bag, you'd do well to patronize either restaurant.

Tortorici's, at 441 Royal Street in the heart of the French Quarter, is housed in the same building in which it was founded in 1900 by Louis Tortorici and his son Anthony, both now deceased. The current owners are brothers Anthony, Jr. and Joe Tortorici, who inherited the business when their father died in 1947. The restaurant has recently been done over in elegant taste and enjoys a local clientele. The menu features excellent Italian cuisine, plus a Festivo Dinner consisting of Shrimp Scampi, baked manicotti, fettucine, Veal Mozzarella, and an Italian salad.

Not all French restaurants are in the French Quarter. Indeed, one that is particularly new and genuinely French is uptown at 2040 St. Charles Avenue. It's so French, in fact, that it resembles the Eiffel Tower in Paris.

Maybe that's because it was once part of that famous landmark. The restaurant's name is Le Tour Eiffel, and the owners are Frenchmen, Jean Onorie and Honor Chef Daniel Bonnot. The decor is part of the original restaurant on the second level of the Eiffel Tower which was sold in 1981. It had become too old, too heavy, and too expensive to restore in splendor during a renovation of the Tower. The original Eiffel Tower had been built as a symbol of the world's fair in Paris in 1889. So Messieurs Onorie and Bonnot had an opportunity to buy the discarded decor and did so. And where else to establish a Tour Eiffel Restaurant but in New Orleans, founded as a French colony by Jean Baptiste la Moyne, Sieur de Bienville in 1718.

It took Onorie and Bonnot a long time to get all things packed and shipped to New York for the move to New Orleans. Then they had to reassemble the present structure as a reasonable facsimile of the Eiffel Tower, but it finally opened with a formal reception on November 29, 1986. Tour Eiffel serves genuine French and French Creole New Orleans cuisine for lunch and dinner. It also offers a late-hour menu for night owls who don't like to go directly home and are still looking for "something to eat" after a party.

One must also remember that some of New Orleans' most famous restaurants are to be found not just in the city, but elsewhere in the metropolitan area.

LeRuth's, 636 Franklin Street, Gretna, is a short drive over the Mississippi River Bridge from the center of the city. It has achieved national recognition for its French cuisine in the relatively brief span of its existence. Warren Leruth is the chef-owner, and his sons Larry and Lee, are renowned chefs in their own right, carrying on the long family tradition. After an apprenticeship as a research chef for Anderson-Clayton Foods Division and stints as a cook at Galatoire's and on the cruise ship *Del Sud*, Warren opened his own restaurant on July 10, 1966, in an old-fashioned home done over in elegant taste. Almost from its beginning LeRuth's became a mecca for New Orleans gourmets, who beat a path across the river to its doorstep. Many tributes have been paid LeRuth's in newspaper and magazine articles by local and visiting travel writers, and the *Mobil Guide* has honored the restaurant with a five-star award. LeRuth's serves classic French cuisine, and the menu is subject to change at whim. LeRuth himself is quoted in the restaurant's brochure: "A good chef is never satisfied with what is. He must always seek what might be." And so his menu changes as his tastes change. And always the changes are delightfully different.

Also on that that side of the river, but in the city itself, is Algiers Landing Restaurant. Opened in 1984, this unique dining facility was built to look old, using weathered but sturdy timbers salvaged from other buildings around the city and reassembled on the Algiers riverfront. It's actually built over the water—on pilings—and at times you almost feel like you're drifting with the current. Every room and every seat in the house commands a spectacular view of the Mississippi and the New Orleans skyline, along one of the river's sharpest bends. Owner David Tallichet said "Everyone who comes in asks for a window table, so as a result, we have all six rooms overlooking the water." Algiers Landing specializes in seafood and steaks, and is open for lunch, dinner, and a Sunday brunch at moderate prices. If the restaurant is crowded and you have to wait for a table, you won't be bored looking around at all the antique furnishings or sitting by a homey fireplace in soft chairs. Chances are, however, your wait won't be long: Algiers Landing seats 250 people.

New Orleans also has an old and famous German restaurant, Kolb's, at 125 St. Charles Avenue, in the heart of the downtown business district. Kolb's was founded in 1899, when a couple of young bartenders, Conrad Kolb and Henry Schroeder, pooled their resources and opened a beer tavern. The partnership lasted less than a year; then Kolb bought out Schroeder and expanded the premises into a restaurant, with Mrs. Kolb in the kitchen and Conrad presiding over the bar and dining room with

great affability and savoir-faire. From this humble begin-
ning, Kolb's has acquired several adjoining buildings and
is today one of the largest restaurants in town.

In the food department, Kolb's excels with pig knuckles
and sauerkraut, and Schnitzel a la Kolb, but the skilled
chefs also have a flair with Irish corned beef and cabbage
and French redfish courtbouillon. Lately crayfish bisque
in season has been added as a feature on the menu.

Also in the central business district is the Bon Ton, 401
Magazine Street. Although comparatively small in space,
it is an extremely popular local restaurant featuring pot-
cooked Cajun food. Crayfish dishes are the specialty here.
There is a crayfish dinner (in season) that includes a
crayfish cocktail, crayfish bisque, crayfish omelet, and
crayfish salad. The dessert is bread pudding. Al Pierce,
who has been operating the establishment since April
1953, speaks with a charming Cajun accent, and will tell
you that, despite the restaurant's reputation for crayfish,
other seafood delicacies such as crabmeat dishes, redfish,
and trout are well turned out.

Excellent restaurants also abound in the uptown section of New Orleans. You might check these addresses for
a delicious experience in dining: Commander's Palace;
the Caribbean Room of the Pontchartrain Hotel; The
Versailles; Dunbar's; Pascal's Manale Restaurant; and
Delmonico. In the lakefront area there is Masson's Restaurant Français, 7200 Pontchartrain Boulevard; and a
number of family seafood restaurants at West End.

Commander's Palace, located in the heart of the Garden District at 1403 Washington Avenue, takes its name
from Emile Commander, who in 1880 converted his
spacious residence into a restaurant. Its only similarity to
a palace is a turret on one corner of the roof. The
present proprietors are the brothers and sisters of the
Brennan family—Dick, Ella, Dottie, and John. They have
made extensive improvements on the premises, opening

the upstairs walls by installing large plateglass windows that enable patrons to look out on the Garden District area and the large trees and lush foliage that adorn the patio, where food is also served in good weather. Commander's Palace is also credited with inaugurating the popular Sunday Jazz Brunch with musicians playing soft jazz as they circulate among the diners. (Other restaurants have now copied this practice.) The walls of Commander's entrance hall are decorated with citations from national gourmet magazines to attest to the excellence of the food.

The Caribbean Room of the Pontchartrain Hotel, 2031 St. Charles Avenue, is one of the few hotel restaurants to achieve distinction for its food. The late Ted Patrick (editor of *Holiday)* and Silas Spitzer, in their book *Great Restaurants of America,* selected it as one of only 103 superb places to dine in all of the United States. Some dishes that have achieved fame for the Caribbean Room are Crabmeat Remick (an appetizer), Trout Veronique, Oysters en Brochette, and Mile-High Ice Cream Pie (a dessert).

Dunbar's, 1617 St. Charles Avenue, deserves special mention because its operation is unique. Its Creole dishes are still served in Creole style. Reservations must be made in advance. The door to the restaurant is locked, and one must ring the bell to be admitted by a maid. The guest is then ushered into an old-fashioned parlor (this is probably the only restaurant extant with a parlor) where drinks are served before dinner. After drinks, the maid escorts you to your private table, where dinner is served in table d'hote style on the very best family china and silver. The menu varies from day to day, but one dish, Oysters Dunbar, is always included. This is a rare blend of oysters and artichokes, and whoever created the recipe is assured of a crown in Heaven.

The restaurant is housed in an old family home in the

Lower Garden District. It was founded in 1935 by Corinne Dunbar, a Creole aristocrat whose husband was a semi-invalid. The Depression years were taking their toll on the family finances when Mrs. Dunbar, accustomed to entertaining at dinner socially, decided to extend the practice to the general public, serving them on a discriminating basis in her home. Thus she instituted the policy outlined above: reservations by telephone only, a servant's attendance, serving dinner on exquisite family china and silver. Checks were never presented by the waiters to the customers: the guest was discreetly asked in advance to step to the rear of the hallway and pay his bill.

These customs are still more or less in effect today, although the management changed hands many years ago. James Plauche, another New Orleans aristocrat and a cousin of the Dunbar family, purchased the restaurant in 1956 from Catherine Dunbar, daughter of the founder, who had continued to operate it after her mother's death.

Pascal's Manale Restaurant, 1838 Napoleon Avenue, enjoys a fine reputation with native Orleanians as well as tourists who've been tipped off by friends about its popular Italian-style food. Seafood is the specialty here (the restaurant is credited with creating "Barbecued Shrimp"), but a variety of spaghetti dishes and steaks are also available. Established by the late Frank Manale in 1913, the restaurant passed on to his nephew, Pascal Radosta, Sr., and family. "Pas," as he was affectionately known to friends, mixed his personality with fine food to create the multitudinous clientele the restaurant has today. "Pas" died in 1958 and the restaurant named in his honor is now being operated by his eldest daughter, Mrs. Stephen (Frances R.) DeFelice, who is carrying on her father's tradition of excellent cuisine and service. There is a well-stocked bar, a stand-up oyster bar, private dining rooms—and a wall full of pictures of sports stars and friends.

Delmonico, 1300 St. Charles Avenue, derives its name from the famous restaurant of the same name, popular in New York in the Gay Nineties. The man who founded it in 1895 had been associated with the Manhattan establishment. The ownership changed hands in 1913 when the restaurant was bought by Anthony LaFranca, who kept the Delmonico name. His two daughters, Angela and Rose, carry on a tradition of hospitality and style. Delmonico is best described as a comfortable family restaurant, with a touch of elegance, that serves good substantial New Orleans food. It excels in its seafood dishes, but its steaks are equally good. Ask for a combination salad—you'll find more fresh vegetables in it than you would imagine.

Masson's Restaurant Français, 7200 Pontchartrain Boulevard is what the name implies, an excellent French restaurant. It's off the beaten track for tourists, being near the lakefront, but it's worth the trip. Masson's makes a Gallic gastronomic symphony of marvels of the sea. Indeed, it was the only restaurant in New Orleans to receive an accolade from renowned French chef Raymond Oliver, of the Grand Vefour restaurant in Paris, during his New Orleans visit in 1958. On his return to France he arranged to have the medal of Le Club Gastronomique Prosper Montagne, the highest honor the French can bestow on a chef, pinned on Ernest Masson, Jr., who had prepared his dinner. (The restaurant has also received *Holiday* magazine awards.) Ernest, Jr., is the son of Martha and Ernest Masson who opened the restaurant in 1947 on the same spot where her father, Albert Dubos, had opened a restaurant in 1916. Ernest, Jr.'s brother Albert

Masson, serves as genial host of the establishment. It was his pleasure to greet President Gerald Ford, who dined at Masson's in 1976 during his election campaign.

How about dining in a real plantation? Tchoupitoulas Plantation, 6535 River Road in Avondale, on the west bank of the river, is fifteen miles from Canal Street in New Orleans. It is open for lunch and dinner (except Saturday lunch) daily. The plantation didn't become a restaurant until 1964, although the estate was built in 1812. The present proprietor is Emile Gennaro, who bought the property in July 1977 from McDonald Stephens. The menu features Fresh Trout Supreme, White Veal Chop Stuffed with Oyster Dressing, and Shrimp Creole.

If you're still interested in Italian food, try Tony Angello's Ristorante, 6262 Fleur de Lis Drive, in the Lakeview section of the city. Tony, a native Orleanian, moved to this location in 1972 after establishing a reputation downtown. He serves Roman and Sicilian dishes in complete dinners from 5:30 to 11 P.M. Featured on the menu are lasagna, fried calamari and cannelloni.

Now for a restaurant that's a conversation piece as well as a purveyor of fine food. Here you can simultaneously go to church and practice gluttony, one of the seven deadly sins, if you don't curb your appetite. The name of the restaurant (3835 Iberville Street) is Christian's. It is housed in a structure that was a Lutheran church when established in 1904, but the name refers more to its owner, Christian Ansel, than to a religious denomination. Ansel's family owns Galatoire's Restaurant; Justin Galatoire, Ansel's grandfather, was involved with Galatoire's, and so was Ansel until he opened his own restaurant in Jefferson Parish in 1973. With his partner Henry Bergeron he moved to the abandoned church in June 1977, and the restaurant has been an outstanding success ever since. Because of its unique location, Ansel and Bergeron carefully preserved the character of the church. Diners wait in the vestibule on a church pew. The waiters' station was constructed of pieces of an old altar from another church. The outer walls are lined with cushioned seats (bench style) that are anchored by simulated pews. Still standing in the front of the restaurant is the old church directory. Instead of hours of services and titles of sermons, the bulletin lists appetizers, salads, entrées, and the day's specials. The cuisine is classical French and Louisiana French Creole.

Would you believe a restaurant fabricated entirely in Hong Kong? Such is New Orleans' most lavish Chinese restaurant, located in Poydras Plaza, 601 Loyola Avenue, adjoining the Hyatt Regency Hotel. It's called the Imperial Palace Regency, and it's owned by a second-generation Chinese-American, Lorraine Lee. The restaurant, built in Hong Kong, was shipped piece by piece to New Orleans for reconstruction here. Walls are adorned with intricate carvings and rare gilded artwork, fashioned from one continuous piece of wood, that tells a story. Silk appears in both furnishings and costumes. Velvet cushions of sienna rust complement teakwood chairs. Throughout the dining rooms are exquisite porcelain statuary, antique handpainted screens, inlaid screens, and other touches of the Orient. The menu specializes in Cantonese and Szechuan dishes. The entire kitchen staff is from China, and the waiters are all oriental and costumed in oriental black pajamas. There is also a Pagoda Bar featuring Polynesian and standard American drinks, and a singing pianist is on hand for entertainment.

Another top-rated restaurant is The Versailles, 2100 St. Charles Avenue, housed in an exclusive apartment building called The Carol. The owner-chef is Gunter Preuss, who's been serving haute cuisine at this spot for over fifteen years. He came to New Orleans from the Washington Hilton, then spent five years with the New Orleans Fairmont before branching out on his own. A unique feature of the restaurant—in addition to its award-winning food—is that its dining room, at a slightly elevated level, overlooks fashionable St. Charles Avenue and its busy traffic day and night. Gunter calls his decor "Renaissance Style."

So much for tips on restaurants meriting special mention. But you'll miss a treat if you don't drop into one of the neighborhood restaurants so popular with families accustomed to Creole cooking. It's also a must to drop in at one of the city's numerous oyster bars where you'll have your oysters raw on the half shell, washed down with a foaming schooner of beer; or to test your tastebuds on a steaming dish of red beans and rice, the staple commodity of many Orleanians; or to try a poor boy sandwich—a half loaf of crisp French bread crammed with ham, cheese, roast beef, or a combination of all three, plus the usual trimmings of lettuce, tomatoes, and pickles.

Creole gumbo is, of course, not to be missed. You'll find it on the menu of practically all New Orleans restaurants. There are also two restaurants bearing the name Gumbo Shop—one downtown, one uptown—both owned by restaurateur Bill Roberts. The one downtown, at 630 St. Peter Street in the French Quarter, is the much older of the two (probably twenty-five years). It's been doing so well for so long, Mr. Roberts opened his second Gumbo Shop at 4932 Prytania Street in June 1981. Both are thriving in business. (To leave town without trying a bowlful of gumbo is to commit gastronomic treason.)

In the spring and summer months, another popular gustatory delight is to drive out to West End on Lake Pontchartrain and patronize one of the over-the-water spots that specialize in boiled hard crabs. The scene may strike you as primitive—eating with one's fingers and piling the discarded shells in a heap on the table—but the experience is rewarding to the palate, no matter the means to the end.

A good meal is always followed by coffee, and there's nothing more typical of the city's individuality than its coffee. Creole coffee is never boiled. It is dripped slowly by the French method. It is flavored more often than not by the roasted root of the chicory plant. A French epicure once said of coffee "It should be black as night, strong as love, and hot as hell." The passage of time, however, has mellowed the taste of succeeding generations. Today you can still order "chicory coffee" in most New Orleans restaurants, but the waiter might ask if you prefer New Orleans or "northern" coffee, which is a concession to our increasing tourist trade. The happy medium struck by most restaurants these days is to serve a darker-roast coffee. Equally popular as coffee with chicory, if not more so, is the coffee served at the French Market—half coffee and half hot milk, not boiled together but mixed just before serving. But one thing is certain—the taste of New Orleans coffee is so distinctive that an Orleanian who ventures elsewhere, whether on business or pleasure, is utterly miserable with any other brew.

The ultimate coffee drink is Café Brûlot, a glorification of the bean's purpose in life. This is prepared in flaming splendor at your table-side. A brûlot bowl or chafing dish is used. Into it go brandy, lemon peel, orange, cinnamon sticks, and cloves. After heating, the strong black coffee is ladled into the rest of the ingredients, set afire, and raised on high in a blazing spoon. Then it is poured into special brûlot cups, from which it is sipped in leisurely fashion. It was Mark Twain who, after a sumptuous dinner terminated by Café Brûlot, declared that dining in New Orleans was "as delicious as the less criminal forms of sin."

If you'd care to take a chance, your palate at least may find its paradise on earth. And for a comprehensive study of all New Orleans restaurants with a personal opinion of each, I refer you to a book by my colleague Richard H. Collin, *The New Orleans Restaurant Guide*.

Dining in the open air at the Court of Two Sisters.
*(Courtesy Louisiana Office of Tourism)*

# 6
# Entertainment:
# High Class, Low Down

Light opera was sung in New Orleans as early as 1810, grand opera made its debut at the Orleans Theatre in 1837, and jazz evolved out of the dances and voodoo rites of slaves in Congo Square in the early nineteenth century. Thus New Orleans lays claim to being the birthplace of both opera and jazz in the United States, and scores of Orleanians will argue with you if you don't agree.

But when the average visiting fireman or convention delegate hits town, his sights are set on Bourbon Street, the modern counterpart of the once-infamous Basin Street— the city's formerly-legal "Red Light District" of pimps and prostitutes. Basin Street died in 1917 during World War I when Secretary of the Navy Josephus Daniels decreed that the "Red Light District" must go because it was endangering the health of the military. Mayor Martin Behrman reluctantly complied with the order, but warned prophetically, "Making it illegal isn't going to make it unpopular."

On the other hand, it was World War II that made
Bourbon Street what it is today. What goes on there isn't
illegal—but not by much. In the first nine blocks of
Bourbon Street, before the residential area, the street is
cluttered with jazz clubs, striptease joints (including female impersonators), adult movie theaters, massage parlors, small restaurants, hot dog stands, piano bars, and
T-shirt shops. You name it and you'll find it somewhere
there.

Talent that used to be on Bourbon Street is now in
short supply. Famous musicians like Al Hirt and Pete
Fountain no longer have clubs there. Pete is still in town
with his club in the New Orleans Hilton, but Al seems to
be commuting from Las Vegas to Atlantic City where
dice, roulette, and slot machines are popular pastimes.

However, there is one musician still on Bourbon Street
who is a "must" for any tourist to see. His name is George
Finola and he plays the cornet, an instrument similar to a
trumpet. National critics have hailed him as "the best
cornetist since the famous Bix Beiderbecke." You can
catch George during brunch time at the Court of Two
Sisters where he toots in a trio "featuring George Finola."

But the top tourist draw on Bourbon Street today is
Chris Owens, a beautiful, talented singer-dancer with a
body you wouldn't believe without seeing it. She performs
in her own club at 502 Bourbon Street, and her act is
worth the money. It's done with class. She doesn't strip to
a G-string like other girls on the street. She takes off
enough to increase interest, then puts a straw hat on a
male member of the audience and draws him on stage.
Then she sits him on her knee and sings "Daddy." The
crowd howls for more, but she leaves the rest to your
imagination. Chris is a lady.

Orleanians in the know seldom cross the thresholds of
the striptease joints unless they've got a palpitating visitor

Preservation Hall offers the best traditional New Orleans
jazz in the city. *(Courtesy Greater New Orleans Tourist
& Convention Commission)*

from the hinterlands in tow. They're aware of the "clip"
that's bound to come not only for the high price of
watered-down drinks but also via the B-girl who rushes to
the aid of the party. So Orleanians patronize the jazz and
piano-bar spots where their dollars get a fairer shake.
You'll hear jazz pouring out of doors in many locations as
you wander around the French Quarter. The following
spots, however, are especially recommended:
—Mahogany Hall, 309 Bourbon Street. The Dukes of
Dixieland, a long-time traditional Dixieland band, carries
on its reputation there with new faces, and is still a hit.
—The Third Line Dixieland Band, 327 Bourbon Street.
The band plays in the patio. The entrance to hear the
music is made though an alleyway from the street.
—The Famous Door Club, 339 Bourbon Street. Veteran
bandleader Thomas Jefferson is dead, but his Creole Jazz
Band plays on.

—The Maison Bourbon Club, 641 Bourbon Street. Almost continuous jazz music, matinee and night, may be heard through wide open doors by scores of people on the street.

Jazz is also heard off Bourbon Street in the French Quarter at the Storyland Jazz Club, 1104 Decatur Street. The band plays jazz from its opening hour of 8 P.M. to almost 10 P.M., after which it switches to country-western, rhythm and blues, New Wave, etc.

But the most elegant place to hear jazz is in the ritzy new Meridien Hotel, 614 Canal Street, where French is spoken mostly by the staff. Jazz is played by a different band six nights a week, and the hotel also features a jazz bar and a jazz brunch every Sunday. Voila!

Pete Fountain, although no longer on Bourbon Street, is someone else you shouldn't miss while in town. See him in his own club in the New Orleans Hilton. It seats 500, more than twice the capacity of his Bourbon Street club where he played for more than 20 years. Then he did a few years on television with Lawrence Welk, and still makes periodic trips to Las Vegas to play in a famous casino where he's under contract. He also makes intermittent appearances on "The Tonight Show With Johnny Carson," and a recording company keeps him busy turning out albums. His performances at the Hilton are 10 P.M. Tuesday through Saturday.

Basin Street? You wouldn't know it today. It's now a respectable midtown boulevard. The bawdy houses where jazz flourished in fame, along with Louis Armstrong, are gone. In their place stands a modern, low-cost housing project, featuring rows of neat brick apartment buildings interlaced with playgrounds and green lawns. But crime in that area is now a problem.

There has also been an attempt to convert Basin Street into a sort of Avenue of the Americas. Statues along the middle ground of the double thoroughfare honor Simon

Bolivar, who liberated much of South America from Spain; Benito Juarez, the Mexican national hero; and General Francisco Morazon, the leader of Central American independence. New Orleans has a large Hispanic population, for whom these names will always mean something.

Louis Armstrong? Now there's a name recalled not only in the United States but throughout the wide, wide world. "Satchmo" has now marched in with all those saints, but his memory lives on in his hometown. A park named in his honor, Louis Armstrong Park—landscaped at a cost of approximately $12 million in the cultural center of the city—was dedicated April 15, 1980. A twelve-foot statue of Armstrong is shown with his trumpet in one hand and the ever-present handkerchief (to wipe his brow) in the other. His widow, Mrs. Lucille Armstrong, who came to town for the occasion, had the honor of unveiling it. The park's 14.4 acres contain 119,770 square feet of rippling lagoons, bridges, a theatre, an auditorium, trees, and pleasant promenades.

Louis started on the road to fame in a waif's home in New Orleans, when the superintendent gave him a beat-up, second-hand trumpet in an attempt to find a field of interest for an incorrigible boy born in the city's slums. "Satchmo" later matriculated in the bars and brothels of Basin Street; yet before his death on July 6, 1971, he had been generally acclaimed as the king of jazz trumpeters and one of our country's best goodwill ambassadors to foreign shores.

Other Orleanians whose names are synonymous with the history of jazz are Louis Prima, Jelly Roll Morton, Bunk Johnson, Sidney Bechet, Bix Beiderbecke, Tony Parenti, Oscar "Papa" Celestin, George Lewis, Fats Domino, Armand Hug, Paul Mares, George Girard, and Fats Pichon.

In other fields of entertainment such names as Marguerite Piazza, Norman Treigle, Dorothy Lamour, Connee Boswell, Mary Healy, and Kitty Carlisle are noteworthy.

But if all else fails, there's still Pat O'Brien's, 718 St. Peter, a club that's surely known all over the world, considering the collegians, soldiers, sailors, seamen, convention delegates, and famous VIPs who have visited it—and had fun. Brace yourself for boisterous jollity before you enter. You may have a little difficulty squeezing into the cocktail lounge because every night is something akin to New Year's Eve. Once inside, relax and enjoy it! As the emcee says, "You're in here now, so your reputation's shot to hell anyway!"

It's difficult to describe Pat O'Brien's. There can't be another place like it. The attraction is neither striptease dancers nor Dixieland jazz. The only entertainment is several teams of girl pianists alternating at twin pianos, plus an emcee who takes an intermittent turn singing or telling jokes. Sometimes the jokes, often blue, come so fast a spinster hardly has time to blush. Songfests are encouraged; they're a sure way to loosen the inhibitions of all the patrons. The spark is supplied by the entertainers who might ask a person, "Where are you from?" If the reply is "Oklahoma," they play *Oklahoma* and you can bet all Okies in the audience join in. Somebody else might yell "Texas!" You can imagine the response to *The Eyes of Texas*. So it goes, whether a collegian requests his alma mater song or an old soak insists on *Sweet Adeline*. The girls know them all—or have the music sheets close at hand. They boast they know the state songs of every state in the union and those of the majority of colleges and universities.

The management anticipates pandemonium if the girls are asked for *Dixie* or *Yankee Doodle Dandy,* so they try to discourage such requests as much as possible because partisans of the North and South try to outshout one another. There was a time when ebullient sons of the South would climb on the cocktail tables and give the rebel yell. This was finally forestalled by reducing the tables to postage-stamp size, thus making them hazardous, if not impossible, to climb upon. Besides, it provided space for more customers. Otherwise anything—but anything—goes. Members of the audience are invited up for solos. Thus you're likely to see a sedate schoolteacher from another state, whose behavior in her hometown has been above reproach, up on the podium singing, *I Wish I Could Shimmy Like My Sister Kate,* and going through the motions as well. Or perhaps a staid banker, in town for a convention, might be leading the house in singing his alma mater, waving his drink to keep time.

There's also the possibility of running into celebrities there. Although the late Pat O'Brien, the bar's former co-proprietor, was no kin to Pat O'Brien, the late actor, the two were good friends. The late movie star never failed to call on his namesake when he was in town. He once told me, "I said to that old so-and-so, 'You owe me more than a million dollars for cashing in on my name,' and he'd tell me he was pretty famous, too." The late Sophie Tucker also made Pat's a port of call when she was in New Orleans—as do Robert Mitchum and other luminaries of the screen.

Pat's is also famous for a drink, the Hurricane. It's a concoction of such centrifugal force that an inhibition doesn't stand a chance before it. The recipe is four ounces of rum, two ounces of red-passion-fruit cordial, and the juice of two lemons. It is served in a large glass shaped like a hurricane lamp, the remainder of which is filled with shaved ice and decorated with an orange slice and a cherry at the top. Two of these, and you're headed for the moon.

It's an expensive drink if you keep the large glass it is

served in—and many do. But Pat's has two other bars
with no entertainment where the price of a Hurricane is
slightly lower. In recent years, several other French Quarter bars, taking advantage of the popularity of the Hurricane drink, have been mimicking the original Pat O'Brien
concoction, complete with a similar glass, at cut-rate prices.
But natives will tell you, "Pat's are better."

Creator of the Hurricane drink is Charlie Cantrell who,
at this writing, is still alive and still a business partner in
the establishment. It happened during Prohibition. Charlie,
who was more painstaking than Pat who loved horse-
racing, sort of evolved into the prime mover and purchas-
ing agent for the club. He dealt with the bootleggers for
the liquor. His best bootlegger insisted if he wanted good
Scotch and bourbon, he also had to take rum. But orders
for rum drinks were scarce at Pat's and rum piled up on
the shelves. Something had to be done. The bootlegger
gave him a recipe for rum drinks, and Charlie improved
on one of them. Hence, the four-ounce rum drink: the
Hurricane.

Pat's general manager and part owner with Charlie
today is a comparatively young man named George "Sonny"
Oechner. He is called "Sonny" because he grew up from
adolescence with the business. He now runs it with finesse
in the same operation as before. The business, incidentally, has two other bars besides the entertainment lounge.
One is inside, just off the street, and is called "The Main
Bar." The other is in the picturesque open-air patio, and
is usually packed with tourists in good weather.

Next door to Pat O'Brien's, at 726 St. Peter Street, is
Preservation Hall, a hallowed mecca for jazz buffs who
prefer old-time improvised jazz by old-time black musicians. The founder and guiding light of Preservation Hall
was Allan Jaffe who, in the 1950s, felt traditional Dixieland
Jazz as played by older black musicians was disappearing

in the city of its birth. He took it upon himself to see that it didn't happen. What was needed was a place where the old timers could get together and "jam."

Allan looked around in the French Quarter and finally found a one-room, beat-up former art studio to serve his purpose. He moved the musicians in without dusting a cobweb, and named it Preservation Hall. Today the name is known throughout the world. It also has a road manager to keep up with the bookings.

But, alas, Allan Jaffe is gone. He joined that great number in jazz heaven on March 19, 1986, mourned by every musician in town. He was also eulogized in the press and on TV and radio as a great, unselfish man. The "Third Line" that followed his cortege to the cemetery blocked traffic all along the route.

His widow, Sandra Jaffe, now owns Preservation Hall with three managers on duty. They are Chris Botsford, who also serves as road manager; his wife, Jane; and Resa Lambert. Preservation Hall and its music are carrying on in Allan's memory in the same fashion as before: no paint on the walls, no seats, no drinks, no food, and particularly no air conditioning. There is a modest admission charge.

The rest of the Quarter's entertainment fare is mainly stripshows, more jazz joints, and piano bars.

Without paying for any of the girlie shows, a stroller down Bourbon Street can get a peek at any of the exotic dancers taking it off by simply looking through the doors held open by barkers trying to induce passersby inside by providing a tease to the senses. If you look in enough doors, you can enjoy a composite act just walking along. And the girls do get down to the irreducible minimum in pasties and G-strings. So do the boys in the female-impersonation spots—and at this writing there are three such clubs.

Some years ago, then-District Attorney Jim Garrison conducted a clean-up campaign of Bourbon Street. A decree went out that each girl must retain at least three inches of fringe around the pelvis at the close of her act. The result was a rush on the department stores to fill the demand for fringe. One dancer I interviewed was indignant. Her act consisted of taking a wine bath on stage. "Doesn't every girl take off her clothes to take a bath?" she demanded. "I take five baths a night. Obscenity? Bah! I'm the cleanest girl in town." So if you ever hear of a reform wave engulfing New Orleans, please remember New Orleans has a special type of reform. Other cities might call it "license." For the record, I haven't seen a three-inch strip of fringe in twenty-five years.

Not all entertainment, of course, is confined to the French Quarter. For supper-club acts with a "name" star plus a "name" band, it's the Blue Room of the Fairmont Hotel across Canal Street in the American section. Here you'll see the famous entertainers who make the circuit from New York to Las Vegas to Chicago to Miami Beach.

For class in the performing arts, New Orleans has four buildings available. They are the New Orleans Theatre for the Performing Arts, the Municipal Auditorium, the Saenger Arts Center, Inc., and the Orpheum Theatre. The Performing Arts Theatre is used for operas, ballets, touring theatrical companies, and recitals. The Municipal Auditorium opens up for such large-scale events as circuses, ice shows, rock concerts, and championship fights.

The Orpheum Theatre's main occupant is the New Orleans Symphony Orchestra. The Orpheum, a former vaudeville and movie playhouse, was made as an offer to the symphony they couldn't refuse in 1982. Its location, at 129 University Place just off Canal Street and opposite the Fairmont Hotel, was also enticing. So the orchestra moved over from the Theatre of the Performing Arts to the Orpheum. An inaugural pre-season gala concert was given on September 10, 1982, with then-maestro Philippe Entremont conducting, and famed violinist Itzhak Perlman as soloist, although the work of renovating the theatre was still in progress. Later that season the orchestra toured Europe. The present musical director and conductor is Maxim Shostakovich, son of the renowned Dimitri Shostakovich.

The Saenger Arts Center on busy-busy Canal Street, the city's main stem, is a converted movie theatre, once the finest of its day. It was gutted and remodeled to its former splendor over a two-year period at a cost of more than $2 million. The playhouse, with a seating capacity of 3,000, was opened March 1, 1980 with a personal appearance by Johnny Carson, TV's "Tonight Show" host. Subscription shows of four Broadway plays per season are the top performances offered, but the theatre is also frequently used by lesser touring companies offering Broadway fare, plus one-night stands by rock stars and concerts that cater to young adults. In fact, it's an all-purpose theatre available to any sort of booking.

Opera came naturally to the early Creoles and reached the peak of its popularity in the Gay Nineties and the early twentieth century. But calamity arrived in 1919 when the famous old French Opera House was destroyed by fire. Thereafter opera languished for many years. In 1943, however, a group of opera-lovers headed by the late Walter Loubat founded the New Orleans Opera which, since that time, has presented four or more operas every season. Stars from the Metropolitan Opera or New York City Center, as well as abroad, sing the featured roles; the second leads are filled by talented New Orleans voice teachers or students; the chorus and dancers are locally trained. Many worthwhile productions have resulted from this arrangement, a few of them outstanding. Withal,

it affords opera lovers a means to an end that would be
financially impossible on any other scale. Sell-out performances have occurred under this system.

Spring brings us the annual New Orleans Jazz and
Heritage Festival, founded in 1970. It started with only a
few hundred jazz buffs paying attention, but in 1987 on
its 19th birthday, an estimated 290,000 fans patronized its
10-day run. The festival consists of day and night pro-
grams. The night concerts feature "name" stars and bands
and are held in theatres, clubs, and on the riverboat
*President*.

The Jazz Heritage Fair takes place on two three-day
weekends on the infield park of the Fair Grounds Race
Track. Ten stages are set up for bands playing all types of
music along with jazz. This includes rhythm and blues,
Cajun (Zydeco), ragtime, gospel, folk, country-western,
Afro-Caribbean, and marching bands followed by "Third
Lines," waving umbrellas, dancing, and drinking beer.
It's a wild and wacky experience comparable to Woodstock.

Another diversion for summer visitors as well as
Orleanians is "La Fête de la Nouvelle Orleans," our town's
annual summer festival now in its eighth anniversary
year. It takes place from the 4th of July to July 14,
Bastille Day. Among its features, it has established a
National Festival of Food and Cookery that runs the
whole ten days all over town. This includes a popular
"Kids' Day in the Kitchen," when the chefs permit the
small fry to take over the pots and pans and cook the
dishes.

In 1987 there was also an old-fashioned 4th of July
picnic in the Audubon Park batture area, and night
fireworks over the river opposite the French Quarter.
More events, such as wine-tastings and a champagne
cruise on the river, are planned right up to July 14,
Bastille Day, when the town is turned over to the French.

And, for "Auld Lang Syne," the city began a New Year's Eve celebration a few years ago to rival the one held in New York's Times Square. At the stroke of midnight, an illuminated ball like the one in Times Square, slides down a pole on the roof of the Jackson Brewery, lighting up a large plastic baby symbolic of the new year, and the year itself flashes in big numbers. An orchestra plays from the rooftop over gigantic speakers that can be heard for blocks. The throngs of celebrants jammed elbow-to-elbow in the street below—including thousands of out-of-town partisans for that day's Sugar Bowl game—cheer and exchange well-wishes with their neighbors, and promptly make a beeline for the bars of the adjacent French Quarter to continue the revelry until the wee hours.

The popularity of this celebration grows every year and, to welcome in 1986, 80,000 people spilled over from Jackson Square to the Moon Walk, taking up nearly every available inch of space. What a way to welcome in the New Year!

Bourbon Street pulsates with nightlife around the clock.
*(Courtesy Louisiana Office of Tourism)*

Louisiana shrimp boat moored on the bank of Lake Lafourche at sunset. Hundreds of these boats follow the
bayou south to the Gulf of Mexico during shrimping
season. *(Courtesy Louisiana Office of Tourism)*

# 7

# Sportsman's Paradise

In New Orleans there are no months when you must stay indoors. The trees and grass are always green. There is no season to store golf clubs or haul sailboats out of the water. It's also possible to fish in a different body of water 365 days a year. Do you like to participate in sports or watch them? Is hunting, fishing, golf, tennis, or sailing your preference? Would you rather watch thoroughbred horse races, the New Orleans Saints pro football team, or the sports-crammed period of events that accompanies the annual Sugar Bowl football classic? It's also possible to catch pro football's world championship Super Bowl game here from time to time.

The 1986 game marked the sixth time the city has played host to the extravaganza. New Orleans will be host again, a seventh time, for the Super Bowl game scheduled for January 28, 1990.

But for tourist-participation sports, let's take hunting and fishing first. The waterways adjacent to New Orleans are interlaced with green marshlands filled with native or tropical wildlife, especially aquatic birds. Ducks and geese by the thousands make the area a port of call during the fall and winter months, and good shooting grounds can be reached in an hour from any midtown hotel. One of the bigger difficulties facing duck hunters is how to stay within the limit prescribed by law. Not long ago a state senator served a five-day jail term for possessing twenty-six ducks over the legal limit when a federal game warden caught him, so to speak, feather-handed.

Deer also may be bagged only thirty or forty miles west of New Orleans in the Barataria region. This area abounds in history: it was once the hideout of the elegant pirate Jean Lafitte and his celebrated cutthroat band. Other game includes wild turkey, squirrels, rails, snipe, doves, woodcocks, quail, and rabbits. Basic information on hunting and fishing may be obtained by writing to the Louisiana Wildlife and Fisheries Commission, 400 Royal Street, New Orleans, Louisiana, 70130.

Both freshwater and saltwater fish can be caught or bought within the city limits. Deep-sea fishing requires only short trips out of town. Boats may be rented at Irish Bayou, North Shore, the Rigolets, and Chef Menteur Pass—all adjoining or adjacent to Lake Pontchartrain. At Grand Isle, a good distance west of the city via U.S. Highway 90 and Louisiana Highway 1 along Bayou Lafourche, several tarpon rodeos with scores of prizes are held in the summer months. A mammoth rodeo in July requires a registration fee, and rod-and-reel fishermen are required to possess licenses. Not only tarpon, but also marlin, sailfish, and amberjack are on the eligible list for the contest. You don't need a license to fish with a pole or catch crabs with a net.

Golf, tennis, and sailing go on forever. A tennis tournament is part of the Sugar Bowl's mid-winter carnival of sports. So is a regatta. Dyed-in-the-wool golf addicts even play on Christmas and Mardi Gras. There are four 18-hole public links in City Park on which to tee off. There's also an opportunity to improve their games by watching the pros in action during the annual Greater New Orleans Open in the spring, now sponsored by the USF&G Corporation.

Another eighteen-hole public links course is available in Audubon Park, but here a peculiar setup makes it less desirable. Visitors enjoy only the privilege of using the course. A private club maintains the clubhouse, which is open to members only, so none of the pleasures of the "nineteenth hole" are available to non-members. Others may, however, call up for a starting time.

Both parks also maintain public tennis courts—City Park has forty-four and Audubon Park ten.

If you prefer to ride horses rather than bet on them, it's possible to get yourself a mount at two locations. The Audubon Park Stables, now moved from the park to 150 Arnoult Road in Metairie, rent horses by the hour. Riding may be enjoyed in a rink on the premises or on top of the Mississippi River levee, which is popular with most equestrians. Riding horses are also available in City Park, which contains bridle paths. Call the Crescent Riding Academy for details.

Boats may be rented in City Park for cruising through the lagoons. No boats are available in Audubon Park. Boats for deep-sea fishing may be chartered near the mouth of the Mississippi at Empire and Venice, about seventy miles south of New Orleans on Louisiana Highway 23; or at Grand Isle, 120 miles away. Information on accommodations for big game fishing may be obtained by writing the Wildlife and Fisheries Commission, 400 Royal Street, New Orleans, Louisiana 70130. The phone number is (504) 568-5612.

124 NEW ORLEANS GUIDE

If you arrive in New Orleans by yacht, you can berth it in a slip at the Municipal Yacht Harbor. Accommodations are also available at the Orleans Marina.

Swimming without charge is possible in protected areas with lifeguards on duty along the seven-and-a-half miles of waterfront parks and beaches on Lake Pontchartrain. The designated areas are adjacent to Bayou St. John and the Seabrook Bridge. The lake is also a haven for water skiing and speedboat enthusiasts.

As for spectator sports, New Orleans' finest week is the Sugar Bowl period which begins two days after Christmas and winds up in glory on New Year's Day when the annual football classic is played in the Superdome.

In addition to football, the Sugar Bowl Calendar includes basketball, tennis, and a regatta on Lake Pontchartrain. All events are sponsored by the Mid-Winter Sports Association, a volunteer, non-profit civic organization. Every member buys his own tickets to all events. Basketball, football, and the 1,500-meter race take place in the Superdome.

Although horse racing has no connection with the Sugar Bowl, it also happens to be in full swing during the same period. Mid-winter is midseason for the bangtails at the historic Fair Grounds Race Track which celebrated its centennial year of racing in 1972. The Fair Grounds opens its annual meet the latter part of November and continues through early March, depending on the number of days allotted for each season. Sunday racing, hitherto banned, was given the green light for the 1972—73 season, with the stipulation that the program would not conflict with the hours of church service or the home football games of the New Orleans Saints. The highlights are the New Orleans Handicap and the Louisiana Derby which occur toward the end of the season. But there's plenty of excitement any day for a sportsman with a wager on a horse.

Established in 1872, the Fair Grounds has survived wars, plagues, and financial crises. Horse racing in New Orleans, however, dates back to 1800 as an organized sport, and heaven only knows how long before that, considering the sporting blood of the Creoles. In recent years another racetrack, Jefferson Downs in nearby Jefferson Parish, has scheduled fall and spring meetings which precede and follow the Fair Grounds season. The racing here is at night, under lights, which is a convenience for persons otherwise occupied during the day. After a slow start and several changes of management, the track is now gaining in favor with the public.

New Orleans Fair Grounds.

Other kinds of sports such as dice, roulette, and black-jack flourish in Jefferson Parish from time to time, depending on the political favor of the men in office. They are seldom suppressed entirely. Jefferson Parish always leads the state of Louisiana in taxes paid to the government for federal gambling stamps, although the local authorities are seldom able to find any evidence of gambling. In New Orleans proper it is also possible to place a bet with a bookie over the telephone with little or no difficulty—despite the watchdogs of the law. And the recent legalization of off-track betting in licensed parlors by the legislature is not exepcted to cut too deeply into the pockets of these bookies. The state constitution can and does say "gambling is a vice and shall be suppressed," but Orleanians treat it with the same lip service they paid Prohibition.

Baseball, which had enjoyed professional status with a team in the Southern Association for fifty-nine years, gave up its ghost at the start of the 1960 season. The franchise of the New Orleans Pelicans was sold to Little Rock, Arkansas. Losing games and the competition of big-league games on TV brought on its financial disaster. As already noted, baseball is being revived in the spectacular new Superdome. The Dome's baseball seating arrangement will accomodate 56,596 fans, with thirty-one thousand seats behind home plate and along the foul line. At various times in recent years, some major league teams have played a few of their spring training games in the Dome, and efforts are ongoing to secure a major league franchise for New Orleans.

Indeed, baseball in New Orleans is indelibly engraved in the memory of its devotees by the records hung up by her native sons who've carved their niche in history in the major leagues. Mel Ott, Zeke Bonura, Mel Parnell, Carl Lind, Eddie Morgan, Bill Perrin, Bobby Brown, Johnny

Oulliber, and Rusty Staub are names that come to mind. Oulliber, once a Cleveland shortstop and second-baseman, has probably achieved the greatest career turnabout in the annals of the game. He became president and later chairman of the board of the National Bank of Commerce in New Orleans. And Bobby Brown, a former New York Yankee third-baseman, later became an M.D. after working his way through medical school in off- seasons. Dr. Brown is now the President of baseball's American League.

Boxing, once a popular sport in New Orleans, still

Football action with the New Orleans Saints is a big local favorite.

commands interest when an important match is made. A most important one took place on September 15, 1978. That was the night "The Great One," Muhammad Ali, won the world heavyweight championship for an unprecedented third time. He scored a unanimous decision on the cards of all three judges in a fifteen-round fight with defending champion Leon Spinks, who had won the title from Ali by a fifteen-round decision earlier that year. A crowd of 70,000 persons crammed the Superdome to see the rematch, and the $6 million gate was a record high at that time. Another championship fight was held in the Superdome January 15, 1972, the night before the Super Bowl football game. In that one the defending heavyweight champion Joe Frazier scored a technical knockout against Terry Daniels.

Local promoters also arrange bouts every so often in the Municipal Auditorium and, lately, in the Landmark Hotel in Metairie, featuring some promising up-and-comers in the professional ranks. And would you believe Louisiana was the first state in the union to legalize the sport in 1891? It was! Fight fever reached its peak on September 7, 1892, when "Gentleman Jim" Corbett knocked out John L. Sullivan and was named heavyweight champion of the world at the Old Olympic Club Arena.

New Orleans also had a native son, Pete Herman, who fought his way to the top of the ranks. Pete, a former bantamweight champion of the world, was one of the few fighters ever to win a world's boxing title twice before Ali did it. He won the championship in 1917, lost it in 1920, won it back again in 1921, then lost a decision to Johnny Buff. At that time his eyesight was almost gone. In his last fight in 1922 he couldn't see his opponent except in the clinches. He won, but he knew it was time to hang up the gloves. Pete, now deceased, spent his retirement years operating Pete Herman's Club, a night spot in the French

Quarter. Local friends and out-of-town fans who had never forgotten the little shoeshine boy who grew up to become a buzz saw in the ring, would drop in from time to time to reminisce with him. The late comedian Joe E. Lewis was one who never failed to visit Pete when he played an engagement in town.

During the year 1963 New Orleans had another world's champion, although, alas, his reign was brief. Ralph Dupas won the junior welterweight championship in New Orleans on June 18 but he lost it by a technical knockout to Sandro Mazzinghi in Milan, Italy, on September 7. He is now retired.

Another great champion who hailed from New Orleans was Tony Canzoneri who ruled the lightweight division for about five years in the 1930s. Still another local who went on to ring glory was Willie Pastrano who reigned in the light-heavyweight division from 1963—65. Willie is a favorite among New Orleanians and a familiar face today, frequently putting in appearances at local boxing matches held by the Orleans Parish Criminal Sheriff's Office and other promoters.

Presently, the sport that generates the most excitement in New Orleans is professional football, as played by the New Orleans Saints who are pampered idols of the town. The fantastic attendance record of their fans, even when the Saints are a losing team, have astounded National Football League officials.

Thus wagers on sports, innate in the veins of the Creoles are still prevalent in New Orleans. Hopes and despair still teeter on the speed of a horse's hooves, the fickle turn of a roulette wheel, or the throw of a "Little Joe" or "Ada from Decatur" to make a point in a dice game.

All of which gives substance to another slogan for our town, "Sportsman's Paradise."

The *Delta Queen,* one of the last overnight passenger-carrying sternwheelers on the Mississippi River, is a regular visitor to New Orleans. *(Courtesy The Delta Queen Steamboat Company)*

# 8
# Old Man River

Although New Orleans is a city that loves its Mardi Gras, its jazz, its food and wine, it lives by water. The mighty Mississippi is the city's economic lifeblood. The Port of New Orleans is second only to New York in the value of its foreign commerce and total waterborne tonnage. But while the port has always been Number 1 in our town, it is presently being challenged for its revenue by a recent surge in our tourism. Tourism is booming because visitors can now see the river. And they can now see the river because the port has generously sacrificed several of its dockside warehouses for the development public access to the riverfront.

The view is now open for most of the way between the French Quarter and the former site of the 1984 World's Fair, now occupied by the Rouse Company's Riverwalk. And there will be even more to see in a few years if a massive Aquarium, approved by the voters of New Orleans recently, is built somewhere along that stretch.

Also, the Greater New Orleans Tourist and Convention Commission has been busy drumming up all sorts of festivals, parades, and conventions that have earned New Orleans the sobriquet as a "good party town." Everyone seems to happily reminisce about "the food" and the people "who know how to throw a party."

However, the port still has a lot of things going for it. It represents a direct and indirect economic impact on the economy of Louisiana. It is the state's leading industry. The port physically stretches along both banks of the Mississippi providing fifty-one miles of frontage winding around the city of New Orleans and including Jefferson and St. Bernard parishes. Interlocking waterways provide additional frontage and services for the port.

The river is a blessing, also, in that a water shortage simply cannot happen in New Orleans. The Mississippi, 2,200 feet wide at the foot of Canal Street, flows enough water past that point (an estimated 309 billion gallons a day) to slake the thirst of the entire population of the United States. Orleanians drink this water after it has been purified in the city's reservoirs, where it is run through a battery of twenty-eight filters and then treated with chlorine. Four steam-driven and two electrically driven pumps, with a total capacity of 160 million gallons a day, force water through more than five hundred miles of city mains. There is a popular saying in New Orleans that once a stranger drinks the Mississippi water he'll be back some day for more.

But the river is also something of a bother. The sprawling city rests on sponge-like ground that in many areas is below sea level. Rainfall must be pumped out via an intricate network of canals that drain the streets through a modern sewer system. (Nature douses the city with some fifty-seven inches of rain a year.) A series of pumping stations, strategically located, then lift the water and

propel it into Lake Pontchartrain. One of these outflow
canals is visible to visitors from Broad and Washington
avenues to the lakefront. (A prolonged heavy downpour,
however, still causes a temporary flooding of streets when
the pumping stations system is overtaxed. This occurred
twice recently, when deluges from the sky on May 3,
1978, and April 13, 1980, caused deep flooding—in some
cases lasting more than a day—in low-lying areas of the
city.)

A system of levees eighteen miles on each side of the
east and west banks also helps keep the river away from
our door. Prior to 1935, the flood tides of the ravaging
Mississippi were an almost annual threat to the city's
safety. But since the Bonnet Carré Spillway was constructed
twenty-five miles above the city, the river's menace has
been practically nil. The spillway, a dike-enclosed runway
capable of diverting 250,000 cubic feet of water per
second into Lake Pontchartrain, was opened for the first
time in 1937. On that occasion the river was lowered by
more than three and a half feet. The spillway was again
opened in 1945, 1950, 1973, 1979, and 1983. The decision to open it is left to the U.S. Army Corps of Engineers
who use a gauge at Carrollton Avenue as their criterion.
The gauge is set at the equivalent of the level of the Gulf
of Mexico. When there is a forecast that the water at the
Carrollton gauge will reach the twenty-foot mark, the
engineers order the floodgates opened. (A reading of
twelve feet would inundate the city were it not for the
levees. The average river stage is seven feet above the
mean level of the Gulf.)

The Mississippi is also romantic. Its muddy swirling
waters have provided inspiration for songs, poems, novels, and plays. Daylight, dinner, and moonlight cruises
still provide opportunities for young people to fall in love.
(See Chapter 1 for detailed description of excursion trips

available on the river and Bayou Barataria.)

The river is worth a visit on foot. Stroll along the riverside. There's the possibility of catching the fire tug *Deluge* in one of her fire-fighting demonstrations. It's quite an experience to watch the comparatively small tug go about her business of pumping thousands of gallons of water a minute out of the river in strong, sure sprays capable of battling a rampaging blaze on a ship or dockside warehouse. There's a story told of a little old lady watching the *Deluge* in action for the first time. She turned to her companion and gasped, "I had no idea such a little boat could hold so much water."

For years the riverfront had been devoted almost entirely to shipping and international commerce. But no more. The Moon Walk opposite Jackson Square and the renovation of the French Market have brought the river to the doorstep of many tourists. Further development in the uptown area began with the demolition of more warehouses on the riverfront in preparation for the 1984 World's Fair. That site is now known as the Riverwalk, a collection of expensive clothing shops, arts and crafts shops and booths, and gourmet and fast food restaurants open night and day in summer and winter.

Nearby is the International Rivercenter, a $250 million complex, comprising the New Orleans Hilton, a 30-story, 1,200-room luxury hotel, complete with convention and meeting facilities, and a tennis club. Included in the center is the Cruise Ship Terminal which now plays host to the Bahama Cruise and Sun Lines, as well as the Delta Queen Steamboat Company.

The old "Queen," which underwent extensive renovations before the 1971 season, acquired in 1976 a new and larger sister ship, the *Mississippi Queen,* of steel hull construction with a capacity of 500 passengers compared to the *Delta Queen's* capacity of 192. One or the other of these riverboats embark from New Orleans on overnight cruises on weekly basis during the winter months until May, and then at least once a month thereafter when they are able to move into northern waters after the thaw.

Both boats continue to ply the nineteenth-century water paths first negotiated by vessels of their type—the "Mighty Mississippi" and its tributaries. They churn along just fast enough to get where they're going, but slow enough for their passengers to savor the journey to historical ports of call that make time seem to stop or even run backward to another era.

And there's another little journey you can take free— the Canal Street ferry to Algiers across the Mississippi River. It's a scenic trip to one of the city's recently designated historic districts—Algiers Point. Or you can drive across the $65 million vehicular bridge, also free. Former Governor John McKeithen, shortly after his inauguration on May 5, 1964, kept his campaign promise to remove tolls from both the bridge and ferry.

Take time to look up at the New Orleans skyline on the way back. It's one of the better views of the city. On second thought, do that from the ferry. The bridge is so crowded with cars and trucks, it's dangerous for sightseeing. There's been a clamor for a sister span for the last twenty years, and it looks as if the project may be realized in 1988 or 1989.

Algiers may puzzle you. Actually, it is part of the corporate body of New Orleans, comprising the fifteenth ward of the city's municipal government. There are several explanations for its name. I like to believe its designation was twofold. First, its geographical position relative to New Orleans bears a resemblance to that of Algiers (Algeria, North Africa), to France. Second, during the Spanish domination of New Orleans the section was a depot for slaves brought in from Africa and the West

Indies; thus the abundance of dark-skinned people across
the river gave rise to the term Algiers Point. Algiers today
is enjoying its greatest period of prosperity. Since the
opening of the Mississippi River bridge on October 18,
1958, several new subdivisions have sprouted on its outskirts. The U.S. Navy also maintains a Naval Support
Activity in Algiers, and a Naval Air Station has also been
established on the west side of the river in Belle Chasse.
And now that one can drive across the river in less time
than it takes to reach many of the east-side suburbs, new
homes are mushrooming as fast as concrete can be poured.
Thus after decades of doldrums for Algiers and the west
side (which Orleanians once dismissed as a "jumping-off
place"), many real-estate developers and wise investors
are looking toward the area's potential as a new frontier
in suburban living.

Almost every habitable foot on the east side, exclusive
of marshlands, has now been subdivided and sold. Some
enterprising souls even have plans for further drainage
and reclamation there.

On July 25, 1963, a new tidewater route from the
Inner Harbor Navigation Canal to the Gulf of Mexico,
providing a permanent deepwater channel, was opened
to shipping. This 76-mile outlet cuts 40 miles off the old
110-mile winding trip up the Mississippi. Its official name
is the Mississippi River Gulf Outlet. A new lock larger
than any yet built in the United States is in its final
planning stage to replace the World War I lock now in
existence. Also, a new $100 million berth at France Road
Terminal No. 6 was dedicated by Governor David Treen
in April 1980. Incidentally, Orleanians refer to the Inner
Harbor Navigation Canal simply as the Industrial Canal.

Back in 1923 the Industrial Canal expanded the deepwater frontage for port facilities and industries near the
city's business center. Five-and-a-half miles long, it is the

connecting link between Lake Pontchartrain and the Mississippi River at New Orleans. Part of the canal is also a link in the Intracoastal Waterway system extending from Florida to Texas. There are two turning basins and several slips in the canal proper, plus the lock, to facilitate the passage of vessels from the higher level of the river to the lower-stage lake and intracoastal waterway.

All of which makes New Orleans the gateway of the mid-continent area to Central and South America and the ports of the world. To give an idea of the city's strategic locale, it is estimated the mid-continent area comprises 39.4 percent of the population of the United States, 55.4 percent of the total area, 37.6 percent of the nation's retail sales, 30.1 percent of the nation's manufactured products, 59 percent of the nation's farm products sold and 61 percent of the nation's mined minerals. Statistically the river averages four-tenths of a mile width throughout the harbor. Its depth at midstream is between seventy-five and two hundred feet. A wharfside depth of thirty-six feet or more is maintained at all times.

The port also provides a foreign trade zone—second in the United States—where products from foreign countries may be stored indefinitely, examined, rehandled, assorted, graded, combined, relabeled, processed, and packaged. Duties are paid only if the products enter domestic commerce. The present 17-acre trade zone in the Napoleon Avenue area will be moved to a larger site when a current study of new locations reports its findings. Another useful facility is the public commodity warehouse which is restricted to storage. In addition, the privately owned Continental grain elevator helps to increase New Orleans' export of grain.

King Rex, sovereign of New Orleans' Mardi Gras.
*(Courtesy Louisiana Office of Tourism)*

# 9
# Mardi Gras

The French phrase Mardi Gras means Fat Tuesday, the day before Ash Wednesday, the beginning of Lent. If you want a last long fling before forsaking the pleasures of the flesh for penitential sacrifices, this is the day to do it. The alternate name for Mardi Gras is Carnival, from Latin for "Flesh, farewell!"

To help loosen inhibitions on such a day, don a costume and mask so nobody will know who you are, and fortify yourself with enough liquor not to care if they do. During Mardi Gras it's not unlikely that you will encounter a 250-pound man clad only in a diaper and a safety pin, with a nippled bottle of milk in one hand and a fat cigar in the other, explaining himself with the slogan, "My mom feeds me Pablum." Or a baboon bedecked with lipstick and earrings bearing a sign, "Pat Boone's sister Bab."

In the French Quarter almost anything goes. Several years ago a clever masker wore an expensive white leather

cowboy costume in front. But as he passed and one
looked back, the handsome blond boy was bare as the day
he was born. This ruse has now been adapted by others
wearing sailor suits or whatever. Some of the cleverest
costumes are the result of last-minute thoughts. I remember chuckling at a fellow who wore a raincoat, hip hoots,
and carried an umbrella on one of the brightest, sunniest
days we've ever had. The sign on his back read, "Dissenting
Member of the Weather Bureau."

That's one phase of the Mardi Gras. Mock royalty is
another. Make-believe kings and queens reign over all the
balls and parades. Rex, the Mardi Gras monarch who
waves his scepter over the joy-mad thousands on the final
day, is always a prominent Orleanian, outstanding in civic,
social, and business affairs. Tradition decrees he need not
be wealthy, but it almost always turns out that he is. He is
the only one of the old-line Mardi Gras kings who is
identified by picture and name. The others reign in
anonymous glory for one brief evening, then fade into
their proper status on the marketplace in the morning.
Rex's queen is always a popular debutante of the season.
Her selection is the highest public honor a girl can
receive in her coming-out year, for she receives the accla-
mation of all levels of society on her great day. And she
must make it in her debutante year or the opportunity is
lost forever.

The Rex parade is the climax, the quintessence of the
whole Carnival season. It begins from its den at 10 A.M.
and wends its way down fashionable St. Charles Avenue
to Canal Street which it reaches a little past noon. Its
progress en route is slowed by stops for numerous champagne toasts, including one at Gallier Hall, the former
city hall, where the king receives the key to the city from
the mayor. This is the hour when the joy of the madcap
thousands reaches its peak. The children, almost all in

costume have been brought downtown to wave to the king; visitors and natives alike are hailing the make-believe monarch whose approach brings the city to the wildest pandemonium short of rioting.

The denouement comes at midnight. After the parade of Comus, oldest of the Mardi Gras kings, the kings and queens of Rex and Comus meet in the Municipal Auditorium to proclaim the end of the Carnival season. (Being queen of Comus is considered by some to be a greater social honor than being Rex's queen, but in later years this has been debatable.) The meeting of the two courts, until recently, was witnessed only by a favored few—by invitation only—but now television cameras broadcast the event live between 11:30 P.M. and midnight. Meanwhile, the spirit of Mardi Gras reigns in the streets. It is this spirit in the hearts of all Orleanians, rich and poor, regardless of race, color, or creed, that enables Mardi Gras to endure year after year.

In recent years large numbers of collegians and street people," hell-bent for a weekend similar to Fort Lauderdale during Easter break, have converged on New Orleans for Carnival season's final fling. This has resulted in the mayor's creation of the Mardi Gras Task Force, assisted by a Mardi Gras Coalition of civic groups, to handle the situation. For instance, the city's Task Force distributes 165 portable toilets at strategic locations in the French Quarter and along parade routes. The Coalition also provides first aid stations manned by Tulane medical students. It's an effort to return Mardi Gras to what it used to be—a family affair primarily for New Orleanians, with visitors welcome to participate on the basis of reasonable good behavior, plus the means to provide themselves with food and lodging during their stay.

The Greater New Orleans Tourist and Convention Commission has completed a Mardi Gras Evaluation Report and presented it to the mayor for further consideration and possible action. And the City Council has passed an ordinance to limit and refine the number of parades now being staged during the period of the second Friday before Mardi Gras through Mardi Gras. It is also stipulated that the number of trucks carrying groups of maskers in the Krewe of Orleanians and Krewe of Crescent City parades be gradually reduced. Beginning with the 1976 season the maximum number for the Krewe of Orleanians is one hundred fifty trucks and for the Krewe of Crescent City, seventy-five.

In 1972, the mayor and officials of the police and fire departments met with captains of the parading Carnival krewes to discuss the increasing hazard of parading through the French Quarter. Control of the crowds and the possibility of fire coupled with the difficulty of moving fire department apparatus through the jammed streets were cited as grave perils to the historic section. As a result there have been no parades through the French Quarter since 1972.

The Carnival season has a tradition of dates on which certain balls and parades are held, and the respective krewes cling to their dates with great pride. What with more than sixty Carnival balls being staged during the period, the old-line organizations, because of seniority, have pretty well "locked up" the last ten days. Rex and Comus have exclusive rights to the Big Day itself. In 1951, however, the Rex floats, which take a year to build, burned in an accident and, simultaneously, the Korean conflict took a turn for the worse when the Communist Chinese entered the battle from Manchuria. Because of these two events, the old-line social organizations decided there would be no Mardi Gras. They had precedence on their side because, traditionally, no Mardi Gras is held during war years. But no national emergency had been declared. And when the late Mayor deLesseps S. Morrison received word from the secretary of defense that Mardi Gras should continue as usual, he wasted no-time. He huddled with the heads of the non-socialite organizations and worked out a revised schedule of parades and balls. On Fat Tuesday itself, a king and queen from the armed forces, in lieu of the social register, were chosen to reign over the festivities. As a result, everybody had so much fun that the debris had hardly been swept from the streets before the old-line organizations announced they would resume their parades and balls the following year, despite the fact the Korean "police action" was even more dire when they made their announcement.

In 1933 rain, which is about the worst fate that can befall Mardi Gras, fell so copiously during the forenoon that the Rex Parade was cancelled. But the sun came out in the early afternoon, and truckloads of maskers who had sought shelter under tarpaulins climbed out to grab the spotlight. Although they were routed only on the fringe streets, the gaily-costumed groups were such a hit wherever they drove that a new annual parade was born forthwith. The group is now known as the Elks Krewe of Orleanians because the Elks are the sponsoring organization. This was brought about by an Elk named Chris Valley who was impressed by the elaborately decorated trucks and decided to organize them into an orderly procession for a parade. In 1934 he was so successful with his dry run that he proceeded to convince both the Elks and the city authorities that a Krewe of Orleanians would be an asset to the general revelry. Thus in 1935 the first coordinated procession of the Elks Krewe of Orleanians took place. The decorated trucks now follow directly in the wake of the Rex parade and, with an orphan boy as king, are one of the highlights of the day. The Krewe of Crescent City, also riding on decorated trucks, follows the Elks Krewe of Orleanians.

That Mardi Gras is a city-wide celebration is attested by

the fact that the black populace, now over 50 percent in New Orleans proper, also gets into the act. Their king is Zulu who arrives by boat on the Mississippi River at 7 A.M. He and his retinue of witch doctors, head-hunters, and king's baggagemen debark at the foot of Canal Street. There's also a "Big Shot of Africa" and a "Provident Prince," who sometimes try to outdo the king in raiment. The Zulus blacken their faces and promenade in grass skirts. In the beginning their few floats were beat-up trucks or wagons, but in recent years they've become more genteel to satisfy upper-class blacks who long have frowned on the Zulus' unbridled shenanigans. Today they have as many as 12 or more papier-mâché floats to more or less conform with other parading organizations. Also, their parade now has a set route to follow. It used to be they wandered all over town to any barroom that offered His Majesty a drink. The late, great trumpet player Louis Armstrong came home to New Orleans in 1949 to reign as King Zulu, but his float broke down in late afternoon and he had to abdicate his throne. His widow, Lucille Armstrong, was honored as queen in 1973.

Another phase of the Mardi Gras is the glow within you. Alcohol may perhaps kindle it—for almost everybody sips of the cup that cheers on such a turbulent day—but it's more than that. One feels a tolerance in the air that coaxes one to let go—a presumption that even Mrs. Grundy would understand the "young in heart" on Mardi Gras. A prominent hotel owner of my acquaintance once boasted unabashedly that he sneaked off to dinner with a blonde he had picked up in his cocktail lounge, temporarily deserting his wife. "Only on Mardi Gras would my wife condone it," he explained.

Such revelry and laissez faire go way back, though just when the custom of celebrating the European Mardi Gras began in New Orleans is shrouded in mystery. One tale relates that as soon as the city was founded by Bienville in 1718 an impromptu Mardi Gras celebration was held by his men. It is a fact, however, that several years prior to the founding of the city, a party of French colonizers headed by Bienville's brother, Iberville, camped on the Mississippi River, twelve miles from its mouth. Noting that the date was March 3, 1699—Mardi Gras of that year—Iberville recorded that the location was officially named Point du Mardi Gras. If some observance of the holiday took place, it was the first in Louisiana.

A revival of "Lundi Gras" (Fat Monday before fat Tuesday) took place on March 2, 1987 on the riverfront with the arrival of Rex, King of Carnival. He came in aboard a Coast Guard vessel, escorted downriver by several riverboats, and landed at Spanish Plaza to claim the city as his kingdom for the last 30 hours of Carnival. He was met by Mayor Sidney Barthelemy and high-ranking Coast Guard officials. Greetings and fireworks followed, as well as a dance from 8—11 P.M. with the Neville Brothers band. City officials hope that Lundi Gras, missing from the Carnival Calendar since 1917, is back to stay.

Because the original inhabitants of New Orleans were Latins, it is not surprising that Mardi Gras celebrations became customary soon after the colony was established. These took the form of balls and masquerade dances, with some spontaneous masking in the streets. It was in 1857, however, that the street pageants began to assume their present-day shape. That year the Mistick Krewe of Comus staged its first parade, a scenic torchlight procession built around the theme of Milton's *Paradise Lost*. The word krewe has since been adopted by all Carnival organizations to describe their secret memberships.

Rex, king of the whole Carnival season, made his first appearance in 1872. His krewe was organized as a civic gesture to greet the Grand Duke Alexis of Russia whose

visit happened to coincide with the annual celebration.
The official Mardi Gras song, "If Ever I Cease To Love,"
was a favorite of the duke's, who is said to have become
enamored of a musical-comedy actress named Lydia
Thompson when she was performing in a comedy called
*Bluebeard* in New York. When he heard she was on tour
and headed for a place named New Orleans, it was to
New Orleans he proceeded. When Orleanians learned
that an honest-to-goodness grand duke was en route to
their city, they felt something very special had to be
arranged. Ergo the birth of Rex. The official Mardi Gras
colors—purple, green, and gold—are also credited to the
grand duke's visit. Their significance is purple for justice,
green for faith, gold for power.

Through the years, since the memorable occasion of
the duke's visit, Mardi Gras has just grown. The Knights
of Momus, who now parade traditionally on the Thurs-
day night before Mardi Gras, were born in 1872 the same
year as Rex. Ten years later, the Krewe of Proteus the
fourth of the old-line Mardi Gras monarchs, came into
being. Proteus parades on the Monday night before the
big day.

It took the postwar years of World War II, however, to
open the floodgates. Today there are more than sixty
krewes that stage annual balls and some fifty-odd parades, although, not all of them take place in the downtown district of New Orleans. All this happens within the
ten-day period preceding and including Fat Tuesday. Each
of the organizations or krewes is ruled by a captain, not
the king. The captain serves in the capacity of a chairman
of the board. His word carries the most weight on any
question to come up, including who might be king or
queen of the ball. Royalty reigns for one night only, but
the captain's power carries on from year to year.

The hard core of New Orleans society participates in

only fifteen or sixteen of the sixty-odd balls and only four of the parades. Other celebrants are considered Johnny-come-latelies and are tolerated rather than accepted as fellow compatriots. Yet it frequently happens that new-comers' balls and parades are more lavish than those of the old guard. The latter are inclined to be more conservative. The non-social groups of comparative newcomers— oil executives, financiers, doctors, lawyers, politicians, etc. —plus wealthy citizens of Jewish faith and ancestry who, by tacit agreement, are barred from the secret social societies, are more likely to loosen the purse strings to stage a more elaborate ball and parade than are those whose values rest mainly in a family name.

Thus in the last several years some of the general acclaim of the season for Momus, Proteus, Rex, and Comus has been shifted to a new organization, the Krewe of Bacchus, named after the god of wine. The founders of this group declared that their purpose was "to give the tourists a break" by staging the most spectacular Carnival parade of all, the Sunday night before Mardi Gras. They also decided to forego a ball in favor of a formal supper dance with a name orchestra. Their invitations are also more liberally issued. Bacchus has been in existence only since the 1969 Carnival season when its sensational debut was heightened by the presence of a celebrity-king, the late Danny Kaye. And the krewe has followed up this trump card by importing a celebrity-king every season thus far. In 1970, Raymond Burr (Perry Mason) reigned; in 1971 it was Jim Nabors (Gomer Pyle); in 1972, Phil Harris; and Bob Hope, 1973. With such a glittering array of merry monarchs, plus the Harry James orchestra for dancing (he played for the 1972 and 1973 balls), the populace has come to look upon the Bacchus parade and supper dance as one of the highlights of the season. Glen Campbell, Jackie Gleason, Perry Como, Charlton Heston,

William Shatner, and Henry "The Fonz" Winkler have also reigned.

Bacchus was the first organization to break tradition by having its floats enter the Rivergate Convention Center instead of disbanding outside the Municipal Auditorium. This is an awe-inspiring sight as the huge floats laden with maskers and preceded by horsemen and marching bands enter the Rivergate and shower the formal-attired guests with doubloons and beads and trinkets.

The Krewe of Endymion, organized in 1967, and parading since that year, followed Bacchus as the second organization to move into the Rivergate and forego a Carnival Ball for a dinner dance. But it wasn't until Bacchus broke the ice that Endymion decided to compete with them in splendor. They increased their membership until it became the largest krewe in town. Their parade is more spectacular, has more and larger floats, more lavish costumes, more bands, more "throws," more parade royalty (the queen and dukes roll in the procession on mini-floats), and more than one celebrity in the parade and dinner dance. Endymion rolls on the Saturday night before Mardi Gras, and people wait for hours for the parade to start. And, because of its enormous size, it now rolls into the Superdome instead of the Rivergate for its dinner dance—the "Endymion Extravaganza."

Something else different about Endymion is that each one of its nine hundred members has a chance to be king. Every member writes his name on a piece of paper, which is dropped into a receptacle. The person whose name is drawn out is the king, and the organization's regulations provide that all his expenses be paid. The captain tells me, "He can't spend a dime."

Of the four old-line social krewes—Momus, Proteus, Comus, and Rex—only Rex provides a striking pageant worth craning your neck to see. The other three clubs do their own things in less sensational style.

Another innovation to Mardi Gras is the doubloon. It was introduced by Rex in 1960 and has since spread to all other krewes. Indeed, doubloons have become so popular in New Orleans that hotels, business houses, and even banks have them minted as souvenirs. Some are plastic, some aluminum, and a few are bronze, silver, and even gold. They are about the size of the old silver dollar, maybe a little larger, and several metal merchants are making a fortune minting them in New Orleans. The parade doubloons usually bear the Krewe's insignia on one side and the theme of the parade on the other. They have become so precious as collector's items they are now posing a problem. Young rowdies fight desperately for them because of their resale value to persons collecting a "set" for the season. Sometimes women and children are brushed aside, even injured, in the mad scramble to catch or pick one up when it falls to the ground, which frequently happens. As a result, there's talk of banning the throwing of doubloons from floats.

The approach of a Mardi Gras parade is heralded by the screaming sirens of motorcycle police. Next come the mounted police or other organized horsemen whose steeds step as close as possible to the multitudes lining the streets to clear the way. But as soon as the motorcycles and horsemen move on, the crowd surges forward again. The king's float then moves into view with the monarch seated on a throne, responding with a wave of his scepter to the cheering throngs. Next comes the title float bearing a caption explaining the theme of the parade. Each ball and parade has an overall theme that is carried out in a pageant. Let's suppose, for instance, the parade theme is "Popular Fairy Tales." The floats following the title car may depict *Jack and the Beanstalk, Little Red Riding Hood, The Three Bears,* and so forth. The floats are fashioned of papier-mâché, trimmed in silver and gold leaf to glisten in the sun. If the parade is at night, there are electrically

lighted floats and the flames of the flambeaux carried by
dancing blacks in white smocks and hoods. Huge lions,
elephants, serpents, and flowers may be part of the deco-
rations. Maskers costumed to conform to the title of each
individual float stand at their stations, wearing safety
belts, and toss souvenirs to the crowd.

Parades in New Orleans occur only during the final
twelve days of the Carnival season. The season itself
officially begins on January 6, the twelfth night after
Christmas, with the Ball of the Twelfth Night Revelers,
one of the older socialite balls. However, Carnival balls
may be unofficially staged as early as December 20, if
Mardi Gras is early in the following year, because of the
large number of krewes now prevailing. For instance,
during the 1973 season, sixty-seven balls were held in the
Municipal Auditorium alone. From Twelfth Night on
there is a ball every night, frequently two, in the Municipal Auditorium, where it is possible to lower a partition to
separate one part of the massive building from another.
The date of Mardi Gras varies from year to year, as it is
always forty-eight days before Easter.

A Carnival ball—whose average cost is twenty-five thousand dollars—is staged with all the elaborateness of a
Broadway or Hollywood production. The lights dim, a
spotlight picks up the krewe's insignia high above the
stage, the music starts, the curtain rises, and a pageant
unfolds. In most cases, the previous year's queen and her
court are promenaded out of the wings by gentlemen in
white tie and tails who escort them to seats of honor on
one side of the ballroom. Masked members of the krewe
then pour onto the floor and take seats to review the
tableau to come. The captain appears in a luxurious
sequined or rhinestone-covered costume, greets the guests
with a wave of his arm, and blows a whistle. The show is
on!

The extravagance of the tableau—a pageant depicting a theme—and its length depend on the krewe presenting it. The social krewes usually dispense with the formalities in less than an hour. The non-social ones often present two-hour spectaculars with no restraints on the purse strings or stage effects. The caste system is preserved by the secrecy of the mask. By never revealing their affiliation with any krewe, the secret members of each organization, particularly those who consider themselves of the elite, are able to dodge their business and political obligations by not inviting those whom they think do not belong. The Comus organization follows this rule of secrecy so rigidly that when one of its maskers fell from a float and cracked his skull a few years ago, the captain steadfastly refused to reveal his identity to the newspapers. And Carnival tradition is such that the newspapers didn't press the issue.

The hierarchy of New Orleans society considers only fifteen or sixteen balls out of the sixty to be worth their attention. This poses a problem, because there are approximately forty debutantes each season, and a family's social status is rated by whose daughter is queen of what ball. Rex and Comus balls of course, are the plums most eagerly sought. But they are not easily come by, for there is a lot of backstage bartering, sometimes bickering, as to which family will have priority that season. And it is the fathers, not the mothers, who must wage the backstage fights in the krewe.

The public is kept in the dark; nobody is supposed to know—and indeed few beyond the inner clique do—who'll be Queen of the Mardi Gras. Yet this decision may have been reached a whole year before, when a certain family may have withheld its daughter's debut in a deal to insure that the next time is her turn. Not so for the king inasmuch as he is picked for his civic as well as his social

stature, he is unlikely to be under forty. Indeed, he may
be as old as seventy. Which explains why the legs of the
kings, encased in satin breeches and knee-length hose,
are no match for those of their beautiful consorts.

Will you get to see a Carnival ball? Probably not, unless
you know someone in the organization. (Bacchus and
Endymion are possible, but remember that they have no
balls, just supper dances. However, it's quite a spectacle to
see their brilliantly lighted floats and marching units
enter the Rivergate or the Superdome and separate as
the floats form a backdrop for the decoration of the hall
while the bands and horsemen exit through another
door.) All the balls, no matter the level of society, are
privately financed. This enables the members to invite
only their friends, so unless you're a friend, or a friend of
a friend who has interceded for you, your chances are nil.
There are no tickets of admission. Indeed, there is a story
that a prominent judge—now deceased—who considered
Carnival something sacred and would shudder as if strick-
en with ague if he so much as heard of anyone seeking a
"ticket" to Comus.

Assuming that you do get invited to a Carnival ball, a
few surprises in social etiquette await you. Protocol at
these affairs decrees that the invited guests be spectators,
not participants in the gaiety. You're there to watch the
masked members of the krewe have a good time. To do
so, you are required to wear formal evening clothes:
white tie and tails for the gentlemen if the invitation
reads *de rigueur,* tuxedos if the notation is *formal.*

A lady guest, in addition to her invitation, may receive
what is known as a "call-out card." If she is so favored,
she is separated from her escort on arrival and directed
to a reserved section on the rim of the ballroom floor.
There she sits until the masked dancer who has sent her
the card has her "called out" by a committeeman. She

then takes a turn around the dance floor with the masker, after which he presents her with some trinket, which in Carnival terminology is called a "favor" for the dance. Unless she is expecting another "call out" the girl then returns to her escort, who has been seated alone in another section of the auditorium. If the ball is given by a women's organization the men get called out by masked women and are given a favor.

Favors vary. Most coveted of all is the "krewe favor," a souvenir of the theme of the ball. If the ball has an Arabian theme, the favor may be a rhinestone pin in the form of a camel. Usually only four krewe favors are given out by each masker; the remainder of the souvenirs are less expensive articles of any shape or form. Maskers with a sense of humor, knowing that the mask hides their identity, on occasion have slipped some startled debutante a dead crawfish or a live miniature as a favor. Conversely, men have been known to present expensive jewels to their secret lady loves under the guise of a Carnival trinket.

The decorum of Carnival balls has also been shattered by the presence of movie stars. Dorothy Lamour, a native Orleanian once attracted so much attention at Comus that she stole the spotlight from the queen. The result was that the next year when another movie star was to be guest of the city (the late Linda Darnell), the krewe steadfastly refused to invite her, despite the intercession of the mayor. As it happened, she was detained in Hollywood for extra "takes" anyway. Zsa Zsa Gabor, a visitor during the Mardi Gras season of 1958, created such a sensation at the Ball of Hermes that the captain lost his head when he spotted her seated in a reserved box. The grand march of the royal court was then in progress, a formality so ceremonial the guests customarily stand in homage. Heedless of the lifted eyebrows of the onlookers, the captain deserted his post in the procession to extend his hand to Miss Gabor and escort her through the remainder of the march. Zsa Zsa wore a flaming-red evening gown, which only made the pair more conspicuous.

In 1950, for the first time since the visit of the Grand Duke Alexis in 1872, Mardi Gras again played host to real royalty. The Duke and Duchess of Windsor came to town—and got invited to the Comus ball! Their arrival on Mardi Gras morning, duly heralded in the press several days in advance, caused speculation as to whether a former king of England would bow to a mock king, Comus, when presented before his throne. Suspense mounted as the occasion approached. At last the big moment arrived at midnight on Mardi Gras, and with television cameras whirring and photographers from *Time* and *Life* clicking, the duke bowed formally from the hips and the duchess swept to the floor in a deep curtsy as thunderous applause cascaded through the ballroom.

Mrs. Harry S. Truman and her daughter Margaret were visitors during one Carnival season when Mr. Truman was President of the United States. They, too, were led to the foot of the throne of the mock king at the Moslem Ball and served a glass of champagne with which to toast their majesties. But neither one lifted her glass—someone had goofed in not determining that they were teetotalers.

Sometimes it happens that a symphony concert is scheduled on one side of the Municipal Auditorium while a Carnival ball is in progress on the other. This fate once befell Leopold Stokowski when he was serving as guest conductor of the New Orleans Symphony Orchestra. His sensitive ear picked up a few hot licks of a jazz band going full blast on the other side of the building while he was conducting a classical pianissimo passage. The temperamental maestro stopped the music and stepped to the footlights. He told the audience in a frigid voice, "Since you have paid only one price for a ticket for the benefit of two concerts, we will stop this one and listen to the other." Then he walked off stage in a huff, leaving the audience wondering if he'd come back. He did, after fifteen minutes, and made another speech deploring that such a fine orchestra did not have a hall of its own where it could not be disturbed by a jazz band. Stokowski's outburst not only rated headlines in the New Orleans papers, it also made the wires of the news services sing. Next morning the comparatively obscure jazz leader, the late Russ Papalia, read Stokowski's criticism and was similarly outraged. "What does Stokowski mean I was disturbing him?" he countered. "He had ninety musicians to my thirteen. If anybody was doing any disturbing, he was disturbing *me!*" The wires jumped again, and so it goes!

Mardi Gras is as unpredictable as the weather, but it's always fun—even with a police strike in progress, which occurred in February 1979. Parades in the city proper were banned by the mayor and city council, but nothing could stop many of the krewes from taking their parades to the suburbs of Metairie and Kenner to toss their doubloons, trinkets, and beads.

It's important to note that all parades and balls are privately financed. The city's only extra expense is the cleanup bill. Beer cans and trash pile up after each parade, and the cost to taxpayers is estimated at $500,000 every year. But it is also estimated that Carnival is a $60 million bonanza to New Orleans as a whole. If you plan to catch the next Mardi Gras, and I strongly suggest you do, check the date. It changes every year. You can figure it out yourself by counting back forty-eight days from Easter, which is always the first Sunday following the first full moon after the spring equinox. But you needn't go to that trouble. The people who turn out almanacs and church calendars figure it out for years in advance.

Moreover, railroads, airlines, steamship lines, and tour

agents advertise the date of the festival as it approaches, so you're bound to be informed in time to make plans. And you'll never regret it, although the morning after you may have cause to second the remark once made by Ring Lardner: "I feel like Rex in a state of Comus."

For further reading on Mardi Gras you should try *Mardi Gras: A Pictorial History of Carnival in New Orleans*, by Leonard Huber; *Mardi Gras*, by Robert Tallant; and *Bacchus*, by Myron Tassin, all published by Pelican Publishing Company.

San Francisco, a majestic plantation at Reserve, Louisiana. This manor, built about 1850, was the subject of a novel by Frances Parkinson Keyes entitled *Steamboat Gothic*. *(Courtesy Louisiana Office of Tourism)*

# 10

# Tips for an Itinerary

The statement that follows is not mine: "This is one city where the gap between wealthy tourist and traveler-on-a-shoestring seems unimportant, almost non-existent." That sentence was written by Ora Dodd of the Chicago *Tribune* on May 21, 1972. Y'know something, it's true. The question is: are you a millionaire or on a budget? In either case you can find fun in New Orleans.

Another visiting writer, Jack Gordon of the Fort Worth *Press* described New Orleans as, "The original and still foremost fun city.... Ah, New Orleans! Here is everyone's kind of town." Mr. Gordon was in town when a James Bond film, *Live and Let Die,* was being filmed here in the autumn of 1972.

So how long are you going to be in town? One, two, three, four, or five days? Maybe a couple of weeks? Perhaps you'll be between planes, trains, or buses, or en route to or from a Caribbean cruise and have time only for dinner. If the latter is your lot and you're not on a

budget, Antoine's, Galatoire's, Brennan's, La Louisiane,
Moran's Riverside, Arnaud's, Le Bon Creole, or Begue's—
all in the French Quarter—are worth a visit. This will
afford you a glimpse of Old World architecture as well as
a taste of typical New Orleans cuisine. (See Chapter 5:
**What to Eat and Drink.**)

For a birds-eye view of the city and the Mississippi
River and the Port of New Orleans, you have a choice of
one of three hotel dining rooms: the 41st floor of the
Marriott Hotel; the 11th floor lobby of the Westin Hotel;
and the revolving restaurant, Top of the Dome, in the
Hyatt Regency Hotel.

If you must count pennies and your time is brief, take
the free Canal Street ferry to Algiers across the Mississippi River, or take the St. Charles Avenue trolley for a quick
look at the heart of the city. Dine at a cafeteria, or subsist
on coffee and doughnuts at the French Market. You'll see
a lot of the town that way.

So much for a brief visit. If your stay is to be longer,
permit me to outline a day-to-day itinerary, based on the
length of time you'll be in town—again, on a shoestring
or a fat wallet!

FIRST DAY:
The well-to-do should start with a leisurely breakfast at
Brennan's, 417 Royal Street. It's a New Orleans tradition.
Here you'll not only get an enchanting sight of a garden
courtyard in the French Quarter, but after breakfast
you'll be in the proximity of a long line of fascinating
antique and curio shops through which you may browse.

You're walking, of course, to historic Jackson Square,
only a few blocks away. There you'll see a statue of the
hero of the Battle of New Orleans, General Andrew
Jackson, astride his horse. The square is also surrounded
by famous buildings such as the Pontalba Apartments

(believed to be the first apartment buildings in the U.S.), St. Louis Cathedral, the Cabildo, and the Presbytere. It is also where the French Market begins, and in back of that is the restored old U.S. Mint where a relic of *A Streetcar Named Desire* stands in the Mint's backyard.

On your way back to your hotel you may feel the need of refreshment, for chances are that more time than you think has elapsed on your promenade. If so, a Hurricane in Pat O'Brien's patio, 718 St. Peter Street, or a mint julep in the Court of Two Sisters patio, 613 Royal Street, will give you a lift. Try also to work in a visit to the historical wax museum, Musée Conti, 917 Conti Street, before dinner.

For dinner it's Antoine's, another New Orleans must. You can't go home without the experience. No glamor, no music, no fine silver or china. The venerable old restaurant specializes only in fine food, fine wine, and service— the same policy its proprietor Antoine Alciatore inaugurated when he opened the place in 1840. But your palate will thank you on your exit.

After dinner try one of the famous jazz spots on Bourbon Street. (See Chapter 6: **Entertainment: High Class, Low Down.**) There are, of course, numerous strip shows, but prepare for the old "clip" in most of them. Sometime before beddy-bye, you should have coffee and doughnuts at the French Market. Don't leave town without them!

Even a reasonable facsimile of such a day will enable you to tell your friends you've seen New Orleans.

For those on a limited budget, I would suggest a first stop at the Greater New Orleans Tourist and Convention Commission, 1520 Sugar Bowl Drive on the Poydras Street side of the Superdome (telephone 566-5011). There one can obtain Walking and Driving Tour maps of the city, plus a complimentary cup of coffee to drink while

contemplating what you wish to see. For starters, Jackson
Square, the Moon Walk and the Jackson Brewery are all
in the same area, and all are free for browsing around.

The French Quarter Walking Tour encompasses thirty-
six sites and takes approximately three hours to complete.
An abbreviated version of the tour includes eleven points
of interest that are recommended as especially represent-
ative of the Quarter. The Driving Tour takes in thirty-five
sites and requires roughly three hours. However, the tour
breaks down comfortably into two parts: a tour of twelve
sites that takes about two hours, and a tour of twenty-two
sites that takes about one hour. The first part of the tour
covers some of the city's older neighborhoods and the
area's scenic beauties; the second part brings the visitor
through the Garden District and into modern downtown
New Orleans. Signs posted at strategic points along the
route indicate all left and right turns to assist the driver
in finding the sites. Each sign has a directional arrow with
the commision's gold crown symbol on it.

Along the route you're bound to run into some neighborhood restaurants that are less expensive than those
with famous names. Such restaurants feature the city's
favorite fare, for their customers, most of whom are
natives, have trained palates attuned to New Orleans
cuisine. The food is often very good indeed. For the
evening's entertainment, a stroll down Bourbon Street
from Bienville Street to St. Peter Street will provide one
with a sample of the myriad types of entertainment
available on "The Street" without spending a dime. One
has only to look through the doors of the strip shows and
female-impersonator clubs which the barkers hold open
to entice customers inside. In the same fashion, one can
hear several jazz bands as one walks along. At St. Peter
Street, however, I'd suggest a turn to the right. Walk
approximately a half block and you'll find both Preserva-

tion Hall, featuring old-time jazz musicians, and Pat O'Brien's, an all-time fun spot in which hardly anyone can help enjoying himself. Both are bargains, price-wise, and are "must" spots for the tourist.

SECOND DAY:
For the affluent visitor, it should be a light breakfast in your hotel room, because you're lunching at Galatoire's and must get there early. No reservations are taken. Eager Orleanians make a point of arriving at 11:30 A.M. to hold a table until the rest of their party arrives. Many natives consider Galatoire's the best restaurant in town but, again, don't look for glamor. Its brightly lit and mirrored interior has frequently been compared to a barbershop.

After lunch take a tour of the uptown Garden District. This is the section where the early American colony settled after the Louisiana Purchase. Later, when cotton and sugar plantations brought wealth before the Civil War, they built their elegant town houses. A number of these old homes are well preserved today and are open to public inspection during the annual Spring Fiesta and on other special occasions. The Garden District today is the prestige address of old-line New Orleans society. The exterior of some of these houses can be seen on a sightseeing bus tour that is restricted to certain streets by city ordinance to preserve old homes in the area, or by private automobiles via the New Orleans Driving Tour. The bus tour also includes a drive along the lakefront, where luxurious modern homes now stand in new subdivisions.

Several excellent restaurants are to be found in or near the Garden District for dinner. Commander's Palace, 1403 Washington Avenue, has consistently won *Holiday* magazine's Distinguished Dining Award—as has the Caribbean Room of the Pontchartrain Hotel, 2031 St. Charles Avenue. The latter is operated more in the style of a fine restaurant than the customary hotel dining room. The Versailles, 2100 St. Charles Avenue; Dunbar's, 1716 St. Charles Avenue; and Delmonico, 1300 St. Charles Avenue, are popular for Creole cuisine. Dining at Dunbar's is family style in the grand manner. Reservations at all restaurants should be made in advance.

For after-dinner amusement, it's back to the French Quarter for the Chris Owens show. (See Chapter 6 for entertainment.) For guided nightlife pilgrimages, it's best to inquire at your motel or hotel desk on what you should see, as well the approximate cost of the trip. Perhaps you'll enjoy a "name" act at the Blue Room in the Fairmont Hotel backed by an excellent orchestra. The Blue Room has a cover charge in addition to the cost of food and drinks and tax. But if you have it, spend it; live a little.

For the less affluent, there's the streetcar ride up St. Charles Avenue around the bend of the river to Carrollton Avenue and back downtown. You'll see those antebellum mansions that escaped the bulldozer, plus a glimpse of Audubon Park and and the universities of Tulane and Loyola, all of which border on St. Charles Avenue. You won't see the Mississippi River as the trolley makes the bend but you might see, if you look quickly, the levees that hold the water back. There's also the free Canal Street Ferry at the foot of Canal Street which affords a broad view of the river and port. If you happen to be driving, be sure to visit our cemeteries at the end of Canal Street to see the above-ground tombs and statuary. It's worth the trip.

For food and amusement, if menus and prices are not posted, it's best to inquire before entering; but most tourists are able to make their own decisions based on the appearance of the establishment itself. Who am I to advise the thrifty? They know better.

THIRD DAY:
Be a real tourist. Study your map. Consider its suggestions on what to see. But if you're lazy and prefer a crash course on the city's topography, sip a cocktail at the Top of the Mart in the World Trade Center tower, thirty-three stories high. There is music and the decor is pleasantly posh. My suggestion would be for cocktails just before sundown, when the lights of the city twinkle on at twilight. It's a view to cherish for your memoirs.

That, of course, would be after a late lunch at Mr. B's Bistro, 201 Royal Street, a good, informal restaurant, or at Kolb's, 125 St. Charles Avenue, the city's major German restaurant.

A river cruise and a tour of the harbor might also be a good idea for the afternoon. See detailed information on afternoon river cruises in Chapter 1.

For dinner, if you're in the mood for good old New Orleans Creole cuisine, try Broussard's at 819 Conti Street in the French Quarter. It reopened under new management in 1975 after extensive renovations, and the food and service now complement its lush setting. Or if you prefer a breathtaking view of the Misissippi River and/or the rooftops of the Quarter with your dinner, it's Moran's Riverside, where the restaurant's French Continental and Italian Creole cuisine will also tickle your palate.

For our thrifty friends, other inexpensive attractions in the French Quarter are the museums mentioned in Chapter 3. There are also numerous art galleries, primarily on Royal Street, where one may browse undisturbed without spending a penny. There are also individual artists with their wares hung along the fences around Jackson Square,

and those with the time and money can sit for their
portrait. There is a Flea Market (open only on Saturdays
and Sundays) where some fantastic articles abound.

As for dinner and entertainment, I leave that to you.
Like every city, New Orleans has something for every
purse.

FOURTH DAY:
Did you bring your golf clubs? Tennis racket? Fishing
tackle? Shooting irons? Or racing form? Golf, tennis and
fishing you can have any day in the year, unless it rains.
There are certain seasons for hunting. And two race
tracks—the Fair Grounds and Jefferson Downs—schedule
spring, fall, and winter meets. Moreover, if you're in town
during Sugar Bowl Week, you'll hit the jackpot of a
sailing regatta, tennis, basketball, and the *pièce de résistance,*
the Sugar Bowl football game.

If you're not in a sporting mood but just want to enjoy
the great outdoors, a visit to either Audubon Park or City
Park is a pleasant experience. Audubon Park has a well-
stocked zoo and an area called the River View which
affords a view of the Mississippi from the batture. The
latter is still in the process of improvement. There are
presently two shelter houses and a concrete level on
which to view the river.

City Park, in addition to its municipal golf courses,
houses the New Orleans Museum of Art. The museum
was the only one in the South to exhibit the Treasures of
King Tutankhamun. There are also tennis courts, and
lagoons for boating. Both parks are interlaced with giant
live oaks that are sure to provide a field day for camera
buffs. Both parks are included in sightseeing trips offered
by Orleans Tours.

Will dinner tonight be at another French restaurant?
There's an excellent one named Masson's on the lakefront,

7200 Pontchartrain Boulevard, that'll give you a change of scene. How about another one named Tour Eiffel, 2040 St. Charles Avenue, operated by a couple of Frenchmen straight from Paris—Jean Onorie and Daniel Bonnot, who brought part of the Eiffel Tower with them. No kidding! During renovation of the second level restaurant of the Eiffel Tower in Paris, Onorie and Bonnot bought the decor that was being dismantled. (See Chapter 5, **What to Eat and Drink.**)

Or is your mood more in the Cajun cuisine style? If so, you shouldn't miss the Bon Ton Café, 401 Magazine Street, in an offbeat, midtown sector of the city. The restaurant features crawfish dishes and other seafood delicacies, and has received such acclaim and patronage reservations are almost a necessity.

Those who must watch their dollars carefully can also visit Audubon Park via the St. Charles Avenue streetcar. The French Quarter can also stand a little more exploring, inasmuch as it would take a full week to savor all of its sights, sounds, and aromas.

"Old Man River," the mighty Mississippi, flows by the Quarter just a block from Jackson Square. There's a "Moon Walk" along the levee here, named after former mayor Moon Landrieu in whose administration the walk, complete with convenient benches, was established.

For raw oysters on the half shell or other seafood delights, the Acme Oyster and Seafood House, 724 Iberville Street, rates as tops in the city. There's also a more elite Desire Bar in the Royal Sonesta Hotel that has tables to serve oysters and seafood buffs.

For dinner, try Tujague's, 823 Decatur Street: hearty eating at reasonable prices. One course is always a daily special—a broiled brisket of beef with horseradish sauce. (See Chapter 5: **What to Eat and Drink.**)

Still another possibility, for either lunch, dinner, or

brunch, is Algiers Landing, a new restaurant with an old
look on the west bank of the river. It sits on pilings
directly on the river and across from the French Quarter,
and is conveniently located only a few blocks from the
Canal Street-Algiers Ferry. Algiers Landing is on a sharp
bend of the river and each of its six dining rooms looks
directly out at the water. While you dine, you can also
watch the passing parade of ships from many nations,
along with our own paddlewheelers at various times.
When the ships aren't passing, you have an awesome
ground-level view of the city skyline. The restaurant
specializes in both seafood and steaks, and is moderately-
priced. The view is worth any price!

FIFTH DAY:
If you don't have a car, I'd suggest you get a map of the
area and set out on your own or with your party by
renting one. You can get information on driving tours
from the Tourist Commission, or map out your own.

How about a trip a little ways out of town, say fifty or a
hundred miles? On the city's outskirts, six miles south on
Louisiana Highway 39, in St. Bernard Parish, is the
Chalmette Unit of Jean Lafitte National Historical Park,
site of the Battle of New Orleans. It contains a 110-foot
memorial and observation tower, and an electric map
illustrates the action of the great battle against the British,
fought on January 8, 1815.

Perhaps a River Road plantation tour strikes your fan-
cy. The name "River Road" is used for the highways on
both banks of the Mississippi, and are just what the name
implies. They follow the multitude of curves and bends in
the river and, for much of the way, they run parallel to
the levees themselves.

On the east bank, fourteen and a half miles from the
Huey P. Long Bridge on the right, is Destrehan Manor.
This old house, visible from the road, was built in 1787.

Deep porches on three sides are supported by heavy
Doric columns. The house lies adjacent to the new Hale
Boggs Bridge which spans the river at that point.

Sixteen miles from the Huey Long Bridge, also on the
right, is Ormond. This handsome plantation home was
built in the late eighteenth century. The main building is
two stories, the lower floor of brick, the upper of wood.
The house has a hipped roof with slender cypress
colonnettes above and round brick pillars below. Ormond
has been beautifully restored by private owners.

Twenty miles from the Long Bridge, you will see the
Bonnet Carré Spillway and flood control structure, a dam
one-and-a-half miles long designed to protect New Orleans
and adjacent areas from the overflow of the Mississippi.
This is a sight in itself. When the water level is down, it's
actually possible to drive through the spillway and rejoin
the River Road on the opposite side. However, when the
river is high—primarily during the spring months—water
may be seeping through the spillway gates. The Army
Corps of Engineers will then have the road blocked off
and a detour through the nearby town of Norco will be
necessary.

Thirty-five miles up the road, on the right, is San
Francisco Plantation. It is open to visitors for a slight fee.
The house's strange mixture of Spanish hacienda-like
galleries, French ironwork, and German "gingerbread"
has made this plantation, built in 1850, a startling example of Steamboat Gothic. It's constructed of plastered
brick, with a gallery across the front and halfway around
each side supported by square brick columns.

Houmas House is sixty-six miles up the River Road, on
the right. Built in 1840 the edifice stands today in almost
perfect condition. It is of plastered brick, two-and-a-half
stories high, with fourteen Doric columns rising two stories on three sides.

Four miles farther up, on the right, is the Hermitage,

one of the finest examples of columnar architecture in Louisiana. A splendid brick mansion in the Greek Revival style with original walls of brick between posts, it is entirely encircled with round, white Doric columns, with wooden galleries, upstairs and down. It was built in 1812.

A few miles further, on the right, is Ashland, or Belle Helene. Ashland is a huge house of unusual height surrounded by a colonnade of pillars, eight to a side. The ground floor gallery is paved in tile and brick, and galleries extend nearly twenty feet on each side. In the lower hallway the staircase, built of ancient cypress with mahogany balustrades, stretches toward the attic. Built in 1841, Ashland was one of the great sugar plantations; it is set in a huge horseshoe of live oaks.

Houmas House, located upriver from New Orleans near Burnside, is the classic example of antebellum mansions in Louisiana. (*Courtesy Louisiana Office of Tourism*)

If you choose to start on the west bank of the Mississippi, along Louisiana Highway 18, twenty-one miles after crossing the Huey P. Long Bridge you will see on the right, the Home Place. This is a typical example of Louisiana French Colonial architecture: raised basement, surrounding gallery. The house was built in the early 1800s.

Twenty-five miles from the bridge, on the left, is the Providence Live Oak, the world's largest oak tree. The circumference of its trunk is over thirty-five feet. Its height is 101 feet, its limb spread is 172 feet.

At twenty-nine miles, on the left, is Glendale, more than 150 years old. It's a two-storied, plastered brick home flanked by a pair of pigeonniers.

At thirty-nine miles, on the left, is Evergreen, built about 1840 in Greek Revival style. Notice the outside stairway which mounts to the second floor, and the twelve tall stucco-and-brick columns that support the roof and wide galleries.

At forty miles, on the left, is Whitney, built about 1800, with wide galleries, front and rear, supported by square wooden pillars. Whitney is constructed of mud and moss between beams of cypress—a fine example of the local materials perfectly adapted to climate and location.

At forty-seven miles, on the left, is Oak Alley, open to visitors for a modest fee. Built in the late 1830s, Oak Alley is one of Louisiana's most outstanding mansions and one of the most photographed by national magazines. The house acquired its name from the avenue of twenty-eight oaks leading to the front porch from the river. The style of the house is Greek Revival, with twenty-eight Doric columns, each eight feet in circumference, surrounding the house and upholding a second-floor gallery.

Should you care to continue a further exploration of

the countryside, I suggest you obtain a copy of *The Pelican Guide to Plantation Homes of Louisiana,* published by Pelican Publishing Company of Gretna, Louisiana. A new and expanded edition of the guidebook contains brief histories of more than 240 historic and antebellum homes and more than fifty photographs of architecturally distinctive residences. The volume features an easy-to-follow map to facilitate visiting the homes. Detailed information on the magnificent gardens and floral life in the area may be found in Pelican's *The Pelican Guide to Gardens of Louisiana.*

In Baton Rouge, eighty miles from New Orleans, the sight to see is the State Capitol, completed in 1931 at a cost of five million dollars. Huey P. Long was assassinated in one of its corridors, and his grave, marked by a twelve-foot bronze statue, is on well-kept grounds. *The Pelican Guide to the Louisiana Capitol* is an in-hand guide for on-site inspection, observation, and understanding of the capitol's architecture.

Toward the east of New Orleans, approximately fifty miles from the city, lie the Mississippi Gulf Coast resorts of Waveland Bay St. Louis, Pass Christian, Long Beach, Gulfport, Biloxi Ocean Springs, and Pascagoula. A twenty-eight-mile-long, man-made beach extends from Pass Christian to Ocean Springs. Along its broad expanse are numerous hotels and motels. Many visitors to New Orleans include in their itinerary a trip to the Mississippi Gulf Coast to relax, fish, swim, or play golf. There's also quite a bit of nightlife and many good restaurants in the area.

There's lots to see, do, and eat in and around New Orleans, enough to keep you busy for five days, or a fortnight. Maybe you won't want to leave at all—it's happened to others who quaffed the intoxicating waters of the Mississippi River in "America's Most Interesting City."

# Index

# NOTES

# NOTES